Discover Your Spiritual Destiny was written to help you understand that your destiny is of tremendous importance. Each one of us has the opportunity to make a unique mark on the world and to leave something behind that will continue to support and inspire others long after we are gone.

It is my fondest wish that in some small part, the information provided here will serve as an inspiration to you to live your life to its fullest. You need not believe that to become a truly spiritual person you must embrace sacrifice, obedience, hardship, and poverty, or that you must deny the hopes, dreams, and aspirations you feel in your heart. Through a greater spiritual awareness of your specific destiny and a resolute sense of purpose, you'll create the opportunity to cross over a threshold into a remarkable new existence where life is finally all you dream it can be.

—*Kim O'Neill*

Other Avon Books by
Kim O'Neill

HOW TO TALK WITH YOUR ANGELS

Discover Your Spiritual Destiny

Unlock the Secrets of Your Soul to Build a Better Life

KIM O'NEILL

AVON BOOKS NEW YORK

AVON BOOKS, INC.
1350 Avenue of the Americas
New York, New York 10019

Copyright © 1999 by Kim O'Neill
Inside cover author photo by Evin Thayer Studios
Published by arrangement with the author
Library of Congress Catalog Card Number: 98-94825
ISBN: 0-380-80306-2
www.avonbooks.com

First Avon Books Printing: July 1999

AVON TRADEMARK REG. U.S. PAT. OFF. AND IN OTHER COUNTRIES, MARCA REGISTRADA, HECHO EN U.S.A.

Printed in the U.S.A.

WCD   10 9 8 7 6 5 4 3 2 1

I lovingly dedicate this book to the man who has swept into my life to become such an important part of my destiny. My darling Britt, it is a great joy to have the privilege to live with you as we have in so many past lifetimes, and once again know you as a soul mate, best friend, and dear husband.

Your endless courage and resolute determination to build greater spiritual enlightenment is a steadfast beacon of inspiration to me that brightens my journey on this earthly plane.

Acknowledgments

THE JOURNEY TOWARD one's destiny is truly a miraculous process. I have been blessed to take my journey with a number of extraordinary human and spiritual beings who have shared their luminous energy with me, and by doing so, have inspired me to reach for the stars.

First and foremost, I wish to thank the angels and other spiritual beings for providing me with their exquisite guidance and direction. They allow me the vision of what I can become if I continue to travel purposefully down the path toward greater enlightenment.

I want to acknowledge my wonderful clients, and thank them for placing their precious trust in me to channel for them. I'm continually humbled by their profound courage and unshakable determination to face difficult issues, and their desire to grow spiritually in order to reach the limitless horizons of their potential.

I am very grateful to be represented by literary agent Patricia Teal, who has tremendous generosity of spirit. It is solely through her efforts that I am fortunate enough to be published again. I thankfully acknowledge the wisdom, enlightenment, and creative vision she shares with me, and her unwavering support in helping me fulfill my purpose as a writer.

I am also very honored to be working with my editor, Tia Maggini. Her experienced guidance and attention to detail helps bring clarity and crispness to my writing. Because of her positive enthusiasm, Tia always makes me feel like Sally Field at the Oscars. By the end of every telephone conversation with her, I am saying to myself, "She likes my work! She really likes my work!" This kind of encouragement would thrill any writer.

I was also very fortunate to have the support of my family, which helped make my journey so much easier. I wish to thank Ann Beckman, Michael Beckman, Carolyn Grace, and Jennifer Honea for their affection, thoughtfulness, and encouragement.

I want to thank my friend Ellyne Rice for her wonderful participation in my seminars, and in the numerous signings for my first book, *How to Talk With Your Angels*. I also wish to acknowledge her ongoing encouragement with this project. Her bright, cheerful presence can light up a room.

I'm especially appreciative to my former colleague Karon Glass for having risen to the occasion on a daily basis to keep everything at the office running smoothly.

And perhaps the greatest miracle of all is my new husband, Britt. I want to thank him for understanding how important this project was to me, as I worked seven days a week for months after we first got married, so that I could finish it on time. I want to thank him for cooking for me so I wouldn't have to leave my writing. I want to thank him for rubbing my neck after long days at the computer. I want to thank him for brightening my spirits by telling me I'm beautiful, as I sat working in my thick glasses, mismatched socks, and shapeless bathrobe. I want to thank him for creatively brainstorming with me, and for endlessly listening to discussions of this book each and every day. I want to thank him for his presence at my book signings and at my seminars. I want to thank him for being my partner, my lover, my husband, and my best friend. I want to thank him for being the most blissful part of my destiny.

Life is a banquet and most poor suckers are starving to death!

ROSALIND RUSSELL
Auntie Mame

Contents

Introduction

MY LIFE'S PURPOSE involves two rather extraordinary endeavors. The first is helping people create an inner awareness of their spiritual destiny that will empower them to improve the quality of their lives. The second is teaching people the simple skills necessary to develop tangible relationships with their guardian angels.

Over the past twelve years I have worked to fulfill *my* spiritual destiny by providing private channeling sessions for clients from all over the world, as well as hosting motivational seminars, authoring articles, and writing my first book, *How to Talk With Your Angels*.

My work as a teacher, speaker, author, and channel has allowed me a clear understanding of the role destiny plays in our ability to achieve happiness, fulfillment, and security. It has also allowed me a glimpse of the heavenly plane through my communication with numerous guardian angels and other spiritual beings on behalf of my clients. In fact, I have spent so much time speaking with spiritual beings that I truly feel I exist on both the earthly plane and the heavenly plane simultaneously.

I've been passionately inspired to write this book by the many wonderful people who have come to my office earnestly seeking information about their particular destinies, or what I refer to as the spiritual to-do lists they were meant to accomplish during their lifetimes. From my experience, I have discovered that every human being is literally brimming with far-reaching potential in terms of what he may be able to accomplish. But our potential can only be reached if we awaken to our spiritual destinies, then develop the strength and determination to achieve them.

Quite often, when a client first comes to my office for a private channeling session, he or she describes confusion and frustration about aimlessly drifting through life with no consistent sense of direction, purpose, or self-awareness. Even the most professionally recognized and financially successful clients express feelings of dissatisfaction and boredom, often exclaiming, "My success doesn't mean anything anymore because I feel empty inside," "I have nothing to look forward to," and "Is this all there is?"

In fact, I believe most people remain frightfully ignorant of *where they have been, who they are, where they are going*, and exactly what they *should* and *could* be doing with their lives to create inner peace and contentment.

The ideas behind *Discover Your Spiritual Destiny* are based on a simple message that has been repeated to almost all of my clients in private channeling sessions by the legion of guardian angels with whom I have spoken. The angels have continually spoken about the fact that *all* human beings have the opportunity and responsibility to accomplish extraordinary deeds, no matter how humble their origins. Moreover, we *all* have the inborn ability to achieve great things on behalf of our fellow man because we are actually spiritual beings who periodically travel away from our home in heaven to visit the earthly plane for short physical lifetimes. We are expected to transcend the challenges and hardships we face on the earthly plane and conduct ourselves as heavenly ambassadors, fulfilling our spiritual commitments to ourselves and to others with whom we share relationships.

One of the most riveting observations I have made in my career is that the individuals who are emotionally blocked or withdrawn often develop a chronic condition that I refer to as spiritual amnesia, or the complete memory loss of their destiny.

Spiritual amnesia causes people to agonize over their life's purpose, wallow in dysfunction, and remain ignorant about the issues they need to resolve. Spiritual amnesia also creates within us an anxiety-ridden, gnawing fear of setting higher goals, taking greater risks, meeting new challenges, and opening completely to a personal relationship. This fear has a profound impact on some people, dramatically limiting the scope of their lives until they experience nothing but mediocrity, disappointment, loneliness, and regret.

Accordingly, the most popular topic in my private sessions has always been erasing mediocrity through an awareness of life's work. In fact, many of my clients dream about performing a type of work that will have a positive impact on the lives of other people. However, I have typically found that when an angel does describe a lofty or exalted life's work to a client, he or she immediately feels astonished and intimidated, their knee-jerk reactions are often, ''*I* am supposed to make such a difference in the world? *Me?* Are you *sure* you're talking to the *right person*? *I* could *never* accomplish that!''

It is human nature to revere great accomplishment,

whether it is achieved in athletics, the sciences, law, education, or the creative and performing arts. We marvel at outstanding talent and enterprising initiative. But although we're quick to recognize brilliance or courage in someone else, we're just as quick to tell ourselves that *they* are somehow different from *us*; more gifted, talented, lucky, or enlightened than we.

As human beings, one of our most remarkable and pervasive flaws is our tendency to underestimate our own inborn talents and abilities, and seriously limit what we believe we are capable of accomplishing. If a person is not working toward goals that are challenging and rewarding, he'll be inspired only by feelings of failure and unhappiness. That is why so many people feel emotional, mental, spiritual, and financial discontent and burnout.

One of my favorite quotes perfectly describes how some people settle for mediocrity in their lives. In the movie *Auntie Mame*, actress Rosalind Russell plays a free-spirited a woman who embraces life with vitality and abandon. In a characteristic burst of exuberance, she loudly proclaims, "Life is a banquet, and most poor suckers are starving to death!"

We must learn to take responsibility for our spiritual destiny and become lively, focused, and deliberate participants in our lives, rather than choosing to remain miserable, bored, frustrated spectators. We are to *act* rather than *react*. We must value and make the very most of our lives.

As short-term visitors to the earthly plane, we must move into our life's work *now*. We must resolve issues *now*. We must build satisfying relationships *now*. We must learn to take better care of our physical bodies *now*. We must fully honor and respect the commitments we have made to others *now*. The angels often explain that what we are experiencing *right now* is not the dress rehearsal of our lives. The curtain went up on opening night the moment we were born.

Discover Your Spiritual Destiny was written to help you understand that your destiny is of *tremendous* importance. Each one of us has the opportunity to make our own unique mark on the world and leave something behind that will continue to support and inspire others long after we are gone.

It is also my fondest wish that in some small part, the information provided here will serve as an inspiration to you to live your life to its fullest. You need not believe that to become a truly spiritual person you must embrace sacrifice, obedience, hardship, and poverty, or to deny the hopes, dream, and aspirations you feel in your heart. Through a greater spiritual awareness of your specific destiny and a resolute sense of purpose, you'll create the opportunity to cross over a threshold into a remarkable new existence where life is finally all you dream it can be.

PART
ONE

ও০৩

Your Spiritual Past

ONE

❧❧❧

Reincarnation

IMAGINE YOU'RE PEACEFULLY sleeping, and you've just begun to have a very compelling dream. In your dream, you are embarking on a breathtaking adventure. It is the ultimate out-of-body experience as your soul suddenly escapes the narrow confines of your physical body. You feel an immediate rush of intense, arousing, restorative energy. Physical ailments, illnesses, or health conditions are instantly healed and you feel vitalized by a sense of euphoric abandon you didn't know existed. With peaceful detachment, you gaze lovingly at the physical body you have left behind that has now become an empty shell.

Your attention is focused on a beam of radiant silver light that floods from the opening of a long, beckoning tunnel. The exquisite light coaxes you toward the passageway, which you enter with eager anticipation. Galvanized by sparks of exploding spiritual awareness, and warmly cocooned inside the radiant light, you swiftly and deliberately move through the dark tunnel.

It is only a matter of seconds before you reach your destination, which immediately seems secure and familiar. Your senses have never been as acute. Without any effort, you suddenly see colors more lustrous and luminous than any you've ever imagined. Your sense of smell intensifies, flooding your awareness with fragrances that are unknown, but divinely intoxicating.

A potent energy force of radiant light flows effortlessly from your fingertips, empowering you to heal, recharge, and strengthen any living thing you touch. Every subtle vibration of nature resonates within you as your sense of sound is remarkably amplified. You possess the keen ability to clearly recognize the whispering flutter of butterfly wings, the lilting rhythm of flower petals as they take flight in a soft spring breeze, and the ethereal splendor of an angel's voice providing solace to those in need throughout the universe.

Prevailing confusion over relationships, life's work, health, and financial issues unravel, and you understand each facet of your life with clarity. All the hurt you have previously encountered in your relationships is released, erasing the memories that can sadden or depress. Feelings of anger and betrayal painlessly fall away like so many grains of sand slipping through your fingers. You easily forgive everyone who has ever caused disappointment or disillusionment. You rejoice to discover that you've left behind all the suffering, turmoil, sacrifice, and melodrama of your current existence. You bask in a sense of peace that is absolute and eternal.

As the dream continues to unfold, you are embraced by a fragrant, caressing breeze that gently focuses your attention on the physical environment. A silvery mist clings to distant mountain peaks, whose majestic heights are partially concealed under a thick, pristine blanket of snow. Lakes, rivers, and oceans flow clear and unpolluted. Flowers grow wild and profuse in brilliant hues.

A resplendent variety of fruit and shade trees provide a refreshing canopy for the sweeping expanse of emerald highlands. Spectacular sunsets splash the darkening horizon with ravishing, illuminating color. All species of animals peacefully share this existence and roam freely, bestowing a magical companionship for those who wish to interact with them.

The beauty of your surroundings begins to inspire an intense longing for a heart, mind, body and soul relationship with another being you could love with all your heart. Instantaneously, you have the power to manifest your soul mate, who is the embodiment of unconditional love. Your soul mate expresses a desire to be your steadfast companion and is willing to make the commitment to remain by your side and cherish you for all eternity. If you begin to yearn for a child, you may call upon the same ability to manifest by simply focusing on what you want and then wishing for it to appear. Friends and family members who also exist in this place soon emerge to join you as a part of your new life in trusting, healthy, stress-free relationships.

Before you made the journey in your dream, creating this level of complete spiritual peace and joy would have been an impossible fantasy. In your dream, however, you've discovered the ability to find true paradise and you have the profound desire to remain there in everlasting happiness.

The dream is but a tiny glimpse of what you'll tangibly experience when your physical body expires and your soul makes the journey back to heaven. The process by which the soul journeys between heaven and earth is called reincarnation.

Heaven and earth make up the two realms of existence in the universe. Our true home is actually in heaven, where we spend much of our time. We are simply visitors to the earthly plane, enjoying short physical lifetimes in order to grow and evolve spiritually, as well as to heighten our wisdom, enlightenment, and maturity.

The true essence, or core, of your being is the soul. Your soul is like a very sophisticated computer with an unlimited memory. The soul records all the experiences of each earthly lifetime. Without exception, every single one of your experiences, no matter how small or seemingly insignificant, is recorded and maintained in the soul's memory bank. The soul's memory bank also contains up-to-the-minute information about your *current* lifetime, including the exact nature of your life's work, the issues you are meant to resolve, and the purpose of your important relationships.

Unlike other computer systems, however, the soul's memory bank is never temperamental, nor does it abruptly lose data, lack room for more storage of information, or become obsolete. It is not sensitive to extreme temperatures, viruses, or unexpected power outages; nor is it necessary to try to decipher a bewildering manual to use it. The soul's memory bank is by far the most user-friendly computer system in existence.

Your soul is very similar to computer hardware. While you lived in heaven before you had experienced any earthly lifetimes, your soul was an empty vessel waiting to be programmed. All the events occurring during each of your earthly lifetimes now make up your computer software, because it is your earthly learning experiences that program your soul's computer.

Impervious to disease or injury, your soul never loses power, or life. Your soul is immortal, and remains fully alive and functioning on both the heavenly and earthly planes of existence. During the process of reincarnation, the soul is the part of us that makes the journey between heaven and earth, and then from earth to heaven, over and over again.

Reincarnation is experienced not only by human

souls, but by animal souls as well. For a human being, it is a remarkably different experience for the soul to return to the heavenly plane than it is to return to the earthly plane. Unlike being reborn on the earthly plane, returning to the heavenly plane is the easiest, most comfortable journey you will ever make.

It is ironic that so many people fear relinquishing their physical bodies at the time of death to allow their souls to once again make the transition back to heaven where they live in peace, harmony, and fulfillment.

You're probably thinking that the existence of a delightful afterlife is a truth that you can't be certain of until you actually make the trip, and then it's too late to change your mind about the departure! And if you're like most people, you might also be questioning the fact that, if heaven truly exists, and you've actually lived there and found it to be such an unbelievably fabulous place, how could you have possibly *forgotten?*

You'd never forget you love your children, would you? Or how much you care for your significant other? Or your pets? The very idea of forgetting someone or something that brings you so much joy seems utterly impossible.

The reason we forget everything we know about heaven and the afterlife is because we lose touch with our soul's memory bank while still in childhood, triggering the onset of spiritual amnesia.

Very young children are the most spiritually pure beings on the earthly plane, still embodying the heavenly philosophy of naturally relating to others with honest emotion, open affection, and total acceptance. But soon after we arrive back to the earthly plane, we find ourselves exposed to an enormous amount of unpredictability, violence, abuse, and all sorts of other dysfunction that causes damage to our spiritual sensibilities and awareness. When this emotional and spiritual upheaval occurs, many children start to become withdrawn, confused, angry, and full of self-doubt. It takes years for a child to learn to dismiss the heavenly philosophies and instead embrace earthly prejudice, judgmental distrust, and suspicion toward themselves and others.

As a child is exposed to dysfunction, he loses more and more of his spiritual awareness. This loss of awareness triggers the spiritual amnesia that causes him to forget his real home in heaven, his ongoing relationships with guardian angels, his ability to communicate with deceased family members and friends still living in heaven, and the specific nature of his earthly destiny. In order to escape the assault waged daily on his delicate awareness, a child often develops spiritual amnesia before the age of ten in order to "fit in" with the rest of society on the earthly plane.

Few children are taught to listen to their inner voice, the voice of the soul. We receive information from the soul by way of our *emotional feelings*. Most likely, you know people who are analytical, or left-brained, in terms of how they make decisions and relate to those around them. Individuals who have more mental tendencies than emotional tendencies can be very uncomfortable around others who openly express emotion or affection. They are threatened by emotional displays because they learned as children to deny or hide their natural emotional feelings, affection, and intuitiveness because of the negativity they encountered when they tried to share these emotions with parents, siblings, teachers, or other key people in their lives. As the leading cause of spiritual amnesia, it's a disabling cycle that many people don't even realize exists.

If a parent is uncomfortable expressing emotion, he will teach his children to discount their emotional feelings and intuitiveness because of the belief that those tendencies are frivolous and counterproductive. Instead of nurturing a child emotionally and teaching him to trust in his own feelings, or inner voice, emotionally constipated adults doggedly instruct their offspring to concentrate singly on their *mental thoughts* and to embrace the analytical, humorless behavioral patterns of those older and "wiser" who have already unknowingly developed spiritual amnesia. To receive the positive reinforcement of acceptance, affection, and respect children so crave, they dismiss their loud inner voices to please the "mental" adults around them.

As children, we start to ignore our inner voices until we completely lose touch with our souls, which causes us to forget where we came from, who we are, and the exact nature of our spiritual destiny.

For example, adults who are more mental than emotional in their parenting styles often fail to consider a child's feelings and may unthinkingly bark, "Why did you *do* that? You need to think! You need to use your *head*!" and "How can *you* know what *you* want? You're only a *child*!" and "I don't care about your *feelings*! You'll do it *my* way! *I'm* the adult here!" and "*You* want to start your own business [or be a brain surgeon, ballerina, supreme court justice, writer, pilot, U.S. president, professional athlete, etc.] when you grow up? With *your* grades you'll be lucky to make it through grammar school!" and "Your *feelings* are hurt? So *what*? Stop that *crying*! I don't want people to think you're a sissy!" and "Ignore her, son. You know how *emotional* girls are. Just leave her alone and she'll get over it" and "Of *course* I can't *see* your guardian angels! They can't *talk* to *you*! They live in heaven! And stop repeating what they say! It's sacrilegious!" and "Do I want to hear what *Grandma* talked to *you* about last night? You know she's *dead*! She's in heaven, so she can't talk to *anybody* anymore! And if she could, why would she talk to *you* and not *me*? That's crazy! Go to your room!''

Of course, I certainly don't believe most adults deliberately set out to disable children spiritually or emotionally. Many analytical adults remain unaware that they are following the patterns they learned from their own parents, having long since forgotten how hurtful they found them when they were children.

At this particular time, children are being exposed to frightening levels of dysfunction at increasingly younger ages, in their living environment, from friends, and from the books, magazines, television programs, and films they are allowed to see. I've heard children actually refer to a television set as their baby-sitter. With all the inappropriate and violent programming that can regularly be seen on television, children are exposed to very adult images that are forcing them to grow up earlier than ever before. While still young, children without the benefit of wisdom or experience must somehow understand and participate in a world gone mad with terrorism, drugs, gangs, prejudice, poverty, war, domestic violence, rampant sexuality, and the epidemics of cancer and AIDS. I'm sure you feel a great sympathy and compassion for the children growing up today. But if you look back into your own childhood, you'll remember receiving the same number of negative messages, although they may have centered on different issues.

What a distant memory heaven becomes for a child who is bombarded with all these negative images, and who may also possess an emotionally closed parent. These stressful and bewildering messages are the catalysts that start the process of spiritual amnesia inside a child until he has no memory of heaven, no awareness of his talents and abilities, the issues he is to resolve, or the life's work he is to perform. He becomes a ship without a compass, and that is exactly what makes life such a struggle. It's difficult enough existing on the earthly plane if we know precisely where we are going and how we are going to get there. However, if we've developed spiritual amnesia, life consists of enormous, painful melodrama and the frustration that results from having to learn everything the hard way.

Does this sound like something that's happened to you? If it does, you're in good company! It happens to almost every one of us when we return to the earthly plane. And that is the reason why I have come to refer to earth as the ultimate spiritual boot camp.

When we're children, our inner voices are so loud and unmistakable that they are virtually impossible to ignore. But by the time we're adults, we've become so adept at dismissing what our souls are trying to tell us that we can't even *hear* or *feel* them anymore.

I can assure you that although you may have forgotten the existence of your soul's memory bank, it doesn't mean your soul hasn't been dependably recording and storing your experiences. When you decide to learn how to once again listen to your inner voice, just as you did when you were a child, you'll be able to access all the information stored there to become more self-aware and more skilled at decision-making. I believe the New Age spiritual movement has come into such worldwide popularity because so many people are trying to be true to themselves, living their lives by what they hear from *within*, rather than being told by others how to live, whom to love, and what to feel. In fact, all of the answers you seek about building true happiness, greater spiritual awareness, and unlimited abundance are just inside your own soul waiting to be retrieved.

You may further broaden your spiritual horizons by developing the ability to communicate with your guardian angels, which will significantly add to your existing levels of self-awareness and quality of life. To do so, consider visiting a neighborhood bookstore and reviewing the great number of books with practical advice on how you can easily develop your own channeling ability. My book, *How to Talk With Your Angels*, offers a step by step technique that is simple and easy to follow. You might also consider finding a reputable psychic channel in your area who can give you one-on-one instruction, or seek out a community center that hosts lectures and seminars on spiritual topics where you can learn with others who are also on their spiritual journey.

Accordingly, as you ask for information from within your soul or from your angels, you will reach new levels of enlightenment that will enhance, build upon, or even replace childhood teachings of religious doctrine that may not be working for you or making sense any longer. A great number of my clients, some very religious, ask how they can erase their paralyzing fear of death originally inspired by early religious teachings, which create a confusing and sometimes alarming perception of the true nature of the universe.

When I first began my life's work as a channel and teacher, I still clung to bits and pieces of what I had learned as a child growing up in the Catholic religion. However, over the last twelve years, my spiritual faith has blossomed into a far greater awareness of the universe through communication with numerous of guardian angels and other spiritual beings on behalf of my clients.

What most surprised and enlightened me during the thousands of private channeling sessions I have given is that guardian angels have consistently told me that places such as hell, purgatory, or limbo do not exist.

All of us return to heaven after each earthly lifetime. The angels also emphatically explained that each human being is accountable only to himself once his physical body has expired and he makes the journey back "home" to heaven. Therefore, when you return to heaven, *you* will privately measure how much you accomplished during the just completed earthly lifetime. Each of us judges for ourselves how well we did on earth. Not God, nor any heavenly council, governing body, or guardian angel ever measures how successful a soul has been when it returns to heaven after a physical lifetime on earth. It is the individual's responsibility to take stock of his spiritual triumphs and failures, and this assessment will determine how the individual will make his decisions for future lifetimes on earth.

Therefore, you may rest assured that when your physical body expires, you will return to heaven, along with all the other souls on earth. You will *not* find yourself disgracefully banished to hell, or any other spiritual no-man's land such as purgatory or limbo.

In channeling such a vast number of guardian angels and other spiritual beings who all confirm the same information, I have developed an unshakable faith that heaven, our true home, is waiting for each and every one of us upon the death of our physical body. The fear I had of dying and perhaps not being good enough to get into heaven has completely vanished. To be completely honest, I actually look forward to it!

While I was relieved to learn that hell, purgatory, or limbo do not exist, I suddenly wondered about the fairness of *everybody* going to heaven. What about the people who deliberately kill, rape, and steal? What about the people who commit crimes knowingly against others without any sense of guilt or remorse? What about people like Adolf Hitler who have behaved shockingly during their earthly lifetimes? *They* go to heaven, *too*?

That was indeed a worrisome reality. I suddenly wondered if I was being prejudiced and superior. After all, it just didn't seem quite right, or *fair* somehow, that *anybody* could gain entry to such a special place. Wouldn't dangerous, disturbed, or unsavory people ruin heaven's beautiful ambiance? I have to admit my nose was slightly out of joint at the thought that I could work to be a good person during my lifetime, but yet find myself in the *very same afterlife* as someone who didn't give a flip about "playing nice with the other kids." It's draining and distracting enough to have to deal with truly nasty people here on earth, but interacting with them in *heaven*, too? When I was initially discovering the reality of a heavenly afterlife for all human beings, I wasn't sure if I liked or understood what the angels were telling me, and I didn't hesitate to express my concern and displeasure to them.

My angels gently reminded me that heaven is the home of *all* souls, no matter what their level of spiritual enlightenment. In heaven, all souls interact with one another at the *highest level of their being*, with unconditional love, honesty, trust, and affection. The behavior of a soul on the earthly plane is usually a far cry from how it interacts with other souls in heaven, where there are no issues to resolve or dysfunction to transcend. The angels continued to explain that the entire purpose of visiting the earthly plane is to expand existing levels of enlightenment to more fully embody the selfless virtues of kindness, sympathy, compassion, forgiveness, respect, and nonjudgmental and unconditional love.

The earthly plane is like a spiritual boot camp we choose to visit to prove our mettle by working through unresolved issues and to accomplish a life's work built upon the principle of contributing to the betterment of mankind.

Moreover, the angels explained, each and every one of us has had lifetimes on the earthly plane in which we'd consistently acted *beneath* our level of enlightenment. Lifetimes in which we were knowingly hateful, cruel, insensitive, or prejudiced, even though at the time we knew better because we had already learned the difference between right and wrong. My angels suggested that I look inward to remember the opportunities I'd been given in this current lifetime in which I could have reacted with greater wisdom or maturity; circumstances in which my behavior fell short of my enlightenment. I was flooded with memories of experiences and encounters that occurred as I was still attempting to work through a number of very difficult issues.

As I took stock and objectively considered how I (mis)handled certain situations, I came to the realization that I certainly would react quite differently now, given the same kind of opportunities, because I've reached a greater plateau of spiritual awareness. This concept I could easily understand.

The angels continued to explain that human beings get sidetracked very quickly on the earthly plane and that is what makes it such a burdensome challenge. Although we all have lofty and sweeping spiritual goals when we first arrive on this plane, we often lose sight of our integrity, honesty, and self-respect as we're bombarded with all the negativity on earth. It is the responsibility of each soul to transcend human dysfunction, accomplish his spiritual agenda, and help others do the same.

Once we return to heaven, we are all accountable for our bad behavior on the earthly plane. We alone judge how we measured up to what we expected from ourselves, considering our existing levels of enlightenment. All the issues that were left unresolved are saved on our spiritual to-do list for work in future lifetimes on the earthly plane.

As I thought about my dialogue with the angels, I became puzzled about what they meant by ''bad behavior.'' Were they referring to the appalling remark I once made to my ex-husband about wanting to run him down with my car? Or were they instead referring to the behavior of someone like Adolf Hitler, who knowingly plunged the world into the Holocaust? When I compared my little indiscretions to his heinous crimes, I was suddenly convinced of the innocence and acceptability of my behavior. Just at that moment of self-satisfied reflection, an angel named Arthur abruptly introduced himself and began to speak to me in tones mixed with impatience and annoyance.

ARTHUR: "So, you take no responsibility for *your* actions?"

KIM: "Of course I do. But you can't compare—"

ARTHUR: "Yes, I can. Bad behavior is bad behavior."

KIM: "You consider *all* bad behavior the *same*? But Hitler—"

ARTHUR: "Let's concentrate on *you* for a moment. When you were threatening your ex-husband, weren't you deliberately trying to hurt him?"

KIM: "I was just momentarily angry. I don't think I was *intentionally* trying to hurt him."

ARTHUR: (*Silence*)

KIM: "Well, maybe I was at the time."

ARTHUR: "So you deliberately set out to hurt another human being?"

KIM: "I guess I did."

ARTHUR: "But you appear to feel very badly about it."

KIM: "Yes, I do. I'd never intentionally hurt someone now."

ARTHUR: "You see how one can mature and develop higher enlightenment? And learn to regard others with greater respect and kindness?"

KIM: "Yes, of course."

ARTHUR: "Since his return to heaven, the soul you mentioned before, the one who was known as Adolf Hitler, has reflected and yearns to make amends for the hurt *he* has caused.''

KIM: ''That's impossible! How could he? In a million years he couldn't make up for what he's done! How could he ever be trusted to return to the earthly plane? It's utterly amazing to me that he was accepted into *heaven*!''

ARTHUR: ''Where would you have him go?''

KIM: (*Silence*)

ARTHUR: ''Heaven is the home for *every* soul in the universe. Even someone who wishes to drive over her ex-husband in a two-ton vehicle.''

KIM: (*Laughter*) ''So you're saying that bad behavior is bad behavior? No matter how small or how significant?''

ARTHUR: ''Precisely. Returning to the earthly plane is a wonderful opportunity. Each soul is to take full responsibility to better himself and improve the quality of life on earth, where so many remain struggling and in despair.''

KIM: ''I think I work pretty hard to better myself and increase the level of my enlightenment.''

ARTHUR: ''When you purposely set out to hurt another human being you are not increasing the level of your enlightenment.''

KIM: ''Okay, I see your point. But then someone like Hitler really screwed up!''

ARTHUR: ''Although he caused untold misery in his lifetime, he *did* act at his level of enlightenment.''

KIM: ''*What*?''

ARTHUR: ''He had the abilities of great creativity, intelligence, and leadership. And he had proven himself as an accomplished orator and writer, but beyond those qualities, he was extremely limited. As you may be aware, he was supposed to resolve issues of envy, deceit, abuse, emotional coldness, judgmental prejudice, suspicion, distrust, and insensitivity. He was self-ish to the point of ruthlessness in terms of justifying his racial hatred toward his fellow man. And unfortunately, he *did* behave at his *existing* level of enlightenment, rather than work to achieve greater spirituality, as was hoped. You, on the other hand, are of a much *higher* level than he, and so much more is expected of you spiritually. Hitler had the excuse of lowly enlightenment. You have no such excuse, however trifling your behavior may seem to you.''

KIM: ''I never looked at it that way. So people like Hitler really do have the chance to get into heaven and then come back here to the earthly plane like everyone else?''

ARTHUR: ''Of course! Like every other soul. The earthly plane is the only place for spiritual growth, so it is his only hope for evolving. Eventually, through participating in enough earthly lifetimes, I believe Hitler will become the kind of person who will wish to contribute altruistically to the betterment of mankind.''

KIM: ''So every soul lives in heaven until it can return to visit the earthly plane and try to move forward spiritually?''

ARTHUR: ''Yes. And before you express such judgmental philosophies in the future about another living being, please remember that every soul is worthy and holy because it was created by God. It is the responsibility of each soul to develop its own enlightenment, little by little, as best it can. Without measuring its success or failure by comparison to others!''

KIM: ''I guess I really didn't understand.''

ARTHUR: ''But now you have food for thought! Remember that every day spent on the earthly plane is a gift. It represents a precious opportunity to achieve greater enlightenment. With the passing of each day, focus

on becoming a better person. I ...
that advice.''

Although initially I was very surprised by ...
said, the more I thought about it, the more it n... ...se
to me. Over the years, because I've had the bel.efit of
speaking with numerous guardian angels, heaven now
seems as familiar to me as my home here on earth. I've
come to realize that it is a destination I have reached
after each of my earthly lifetimes. My fear of passing
from the earthly plane has been erased because I have
remembered that heaven is my home, and I know with
a certainty that I will return there, to live in peace, harmony, and fulfillment. And of course, so will you!

If you were raised in a family that practiced a particular religion, you may be wondering about the similarities and differences between religion and spirituality.

Religion is the practice of an organized faith. People
who consider themselves to be religious look toward the
religious leaders in their faith to help them find solutions
to issues and to help them through traumatic situations.
If you consider yourself religious, it means that you are
practicing some or all of the doctrine as established in
an organized religion, and the teachings of that religion
make up your faith and belief system.

Spirituality is the practice of individually observing
and pursuing beliefs without restrictions or regulations
of religious dogma or doctrine. Individuals who are spiritual ask for *direct* guidance from God, their angels, or
their own souls when seeking solutions to difficult problems. If you consider yourself to be more spiritual than
religious, you have moved away from the practices of
an organized religion. You are instead reestablishing
your spiritual beliefs, philosophies, and sensibilities
based upon your inner voice, emotional feelings, and

very likely direct angelic guidance about what is right for you.

Although the intent of this book is to *spiritually* widen your horizons about the true nature of the universe, let me also state that in no way am I suggesting you discount or dismiss any religious philosophy you now embrace, if those beliefs are supporting you in building and maintaining a spectacular quality of life.

Religious beliefs and traditions can be a very uplifting, comforting resource during difficult or traumatic periods, and I want to recognize the legions of pious clergy members who work tirelessly to provide solace to their fellow man.

However, I find it confounding when I hear people who are religiously devout admit to having a great fear of death because they remain anxious and uncertain about what fate will await them when their physical body expires. I have come to believe that many religions are responsible for *creating* and *perpetuating* the fear and insecurity of death and the afterlife because they provide mixed messages that serve to confuse rather than enlighten.

How is that confusion possible, when almost *all* religions fully embrace the philosophy of a heavenly afterlife, as well as the existence of God and angelic beings who guide and protect those on the earthly plane? Why are people so insecure and afraid about what they'll encounter in the afterlife when almost all organized religions confirm the existence of heaven?

I believe a large part of the confusion begins when we're exposed to various and sundry messages about dying and the possibility of being forced to spend all eternity in a spiritual no-man's land like limbo, or worse, going to hell, because heaven is a closed club that doesn't want us as a new member!

Of course, there are those people who don't trust in

the existence of God, or angels, or subscribe to the afterlife theory at all, people who believe that once the physical body expires, the soul is plunged into a black void of empty nothingness. If a person truly believes that this life on the spiritual boot camp of earth is *all there is*, or that it might actually be *better* than what he is going to experience in the afterlife, he certainly doesn't have much to look forward to, does he?

Reincarnation serves to contradict many of the western religious philosophies because of its three basic principles. First, that each soul continues to live after the demise of its earthly physical body. Second, that each soul continues to journey between heaven and earth, and that each soul returns to *heaven* after each of its lifetimes on earth. And third, upon returning to heaven, each soul *personally* measures the level of success it has achieved in the just completed earthly lifetime, unencumbered by spiritual penalties, punishment or liability.

Therefore, reincarnation may be colorfully described as spiritual genealogy. Your *existing* gifts, talents, and abilities reflect not only what you have accomplished and experienced thus far in your *current* lifetime, but instead, is the sum total of what you have achieved in *all of your previous lives* as well. Becoming acquainted with your past life history will allow you to significantly raise the expectations you set for yourself and the ultimate quality of life you hope to achieve. You'll open doors to a heightened self-awareness and a more realistic assessment of the previously earned talents and abilities you didn't know existed.

Aren't you curious about your own past lifetimes? If you decide to explore your unique past life history, you'll be able to discover exactly what you achieved previous to your current lifetime. Past life experiences contribute to your existing levels of enlightenment because they create the framework for your current talents, abilities, passions, tastes, fears, and foibles.

Your ability to channel also validates the reality of heaven and the existence of its spiritual inhabitants. Channeling is the process of communication that takes place between spiritual beings living in heaven and human beings living on the earthly plane.

All the residents of heaven, including God, the network of guardian angels, and "deceased" humans are spiritual beings. They regularly provide humans with a wealth of intuitive insight designed to help pave the way for success and fulfillment. We receive messages from these spiritual beings during waking hours and while we sleep.

During waking hours, your angels speak to you telepathically, providing intuitive information that sounds like a little voice inside your head, which you very likely interpret as *your own thoughts*. While you're asleep, angels and other spiritual beings communicate with you in the form of dreams, which are meant to provide insight into your career, relationships, health, and even safety.

Think for a moment about the dreams you've had that have been particularly memorable or repetitive. Along with recalling past-life experiences, your dreams bring clarity to what is happening currently in your life, and even furnish an awareness of what is to come in the future. It may also prove very comforting for deceased friends and family members to maintain a relationship with you by making an appearance in your dreams, often to dispense some very necessary information that they feel will be spiritually constructive.

Moreover, each and every human being has at least two guardian angels assigned to them. When an individual is open to spiritual communication, or going through a period of stressful transition, there are often a far greater number of angels working with him to provide assistance and direction.

Guardian angels start to communicate with us when we're tiny babies and continue to provide unwavering support throughout our lives, even if we remain unaware of their existence, or our own ability to speak with them. In order to work together more cohesively, we must become aware of their presence and learn to listen to what they reveal with greater sensitivity.

Developing the ability to channel your angels will dramatically improve your quality of life. Your angels can give you direction, speed up your progress, and allow you to avoid unnecessary stumbling blocks.

What I want you to remember is that the process of channeling is incredibly *easy*. While it may sound grandiose to communicate with heavenly beings, it is your birthright as a full-fledged member of the same community. Don't forget that you, too, are a spiritual being, and live in heaven between each of your earthly lifetimes. You are only here on the earthly plane for a short spiritual pilgrimage to accomplish a number of very specific goals. You are a spiritual being yourself, and have guardian angels already assigned to work with you to assist in the accomplishment of your spiritual agenda. Your guardian angels have been providing intuitive information to you since you were a tiny child, and because this communication has already been occurring, there is no question about your ability to be able to do it. You have *already been channeling* for years, whether you realize it or not. The ability to continue doing so will remain intact no matter how much you ignore or deny that the process is taking place. However, I urge you to work on building your channeling skills, because that alone can have more of an impact on developing your spiritual growth and positive self-awareness than anything else you could do. With just a little practice, you can actually build communication skills that will allow you to have a two-way conversation with your guardian angels or deceased friends and family members whenever and wherever you wish. Imagine how life-changing it would be to have immediate access to the wealth of information available from them and how you could use those insights to build far greater success in your life.

Now you recognize the significance of reincarnation, which is the continual journey between heaven and earth. You also understand that your true home is in heaven, and that heaven will be your only destination after you complete your existing physical lifetime. You are very likely becoming curious about exploring your past lifetimes to get a glimpse of your existing, yet unknown, skills and talents. Your sense of reality has expanded to accept the awareness of your own ability to fully communicate with spiritual beings, including your guardian angels and deceased loved ones. In this moment of spiritual evolution, we're ready to increase your awareness to yet another level. It's time to learn about your spiritual destiny!

TWO

❧❧

Spiritual Destiny

ARE YOU AWARE that the secret to creating inner peace and happiness is directly related to carrying out your spiritual destiny? Think of destiny in terms of a spiritual to-do list. Make no mistake—you are currently living on the earthly plane to accomplish a very specific set of goals and objectives that you planned while you were in heaven. Fulfilling your destiny is the *most important reason* you have been reborn on the earthly plane, and your *entire quality of life* hinges on how you pursue your spiritual objectives.

The secret of happiness and a blissful quality of life is twofold. It is both the awareness of one's spiritual destiny and the daily commitment one makes to fulfill it.

I promise this isn't as difficult as it sounds. If it were that arduous or complicated, no one would be able to achieve it! In truth, spiritual destiny is a very simple concept.

Imagine taking some time off from your busy schedule to embark on a long-distance trip. This journey will

25

allow you to experience emotional passion, new levels of professional achievement, romantic adventure, and the opportunity to profoundly improve the quality of other people's lives. You've chosen an exotic, exciting vacation spot you've visited before and yearn to experience again.

Pretend that you've just reached your destination. As you go about exploring, sometimes you choose to take a lingering, more scenic route, deliberately prolonging your enjoyment of a particular area. Other times, you spontaneously decide to travel at a more dynamic pace, and hurry to each place out of curiosity and eager enthusiasm.

During your excursion, you may occasionally encounter an obstacle that may slow your progress or actually derail your journey for a short period of time. For example, you may discover unforeseen changes that have taken place since the last time you visited have caused you to lose your way, and you need to stop and ask for directions (unless you're a man!) to set you back on course. Your vehicle could unexpectedly break down, or you might experience friction from a traveling companion.

But as you persevered, you eventually reached all the points of interest you planned to explore. You were not deterred when your companion became temperamental, your travel plans hit some snags, or because the environment you were visiting was unfamiliar.

As you made your way, eventually the journey became easier, and you felt a sense of confidence and empowerment. Because of your independent and resolute determination, you were ultimately successful in accomplishing your objectives.

Similarly, you may look upon the adventure of embarking on your spiritual destiny as you would a very eventful vacation. You're deliberately scheduling time away from your home in heaven for a journey that will take you to the exciting, unpredictable earthly plane. The itinerary, or spiritual agenda, for your trip is tailored for each successive earthly lifetime. Your destiny actually represents a series of emotional, spiritual, mental, and physical challenges, or destinations, for you to reach on the earthly plane, one right after the other, on a particular schedule. You'll reach some of these destinations alone, but you'll arrive at other destinations with friends and loved ones.

As with any other long-awaited trip, the "vacation" experience on earth is meant to be fully savored and enjoyed *in the moment*. Although by its very nature, it is a destination that serves to frequently challenge you with difficult encounters and intermittent hardships, it is the only place in the universe specifically created to give each visitor the opportunity to triumph over adversity, and in turn, earn spiritual advancement.

Like the heavenly plane, the earthly plane can just as fully support true ongoing happiness, but only if a visitor attempts to live in the moment, can recall his destiny, and maintains the initiative to accomplish his specific destiny by journeying one step at a time toward each new spiritual discovery.

Sadly, while creating happiness is a quest all human beings begin, very few ever succeed in achieving it. Like our ability to communicate with our guardian angels, securing happiness on the earthly plane is a *birthright* for every human being, no matter how lowly our current levels of maturity or enlightenment.

What I am saying, in all certainty, is that no matter how fouled up, miserable, confusing, or dysfunctional your life is now, you have the ability to be happy. And I don't mean the kind of misguided happiness that comes from kidding yourself about your circumstances, deny-ing your problems, or enjoying a false sense of well-being with the newest designer pharmaceuticals. I am referring to attaining a profound, penetrating bliss that you feel each and every day, that can only be achieved by understanding your specific destiny and by being determined to fulfill it.

For centuries, countless books, speeches, paintings, songs, poems, films, operas, ballets, and plays have celebrated the existence of true happiness. If you're an optimist like me, and you reveal to others that you believe in such bliss, you might well be regarded as naïve and misguided, and you'll likely be told that true happiness cannot exist on the earthly plane.

There are many people who regard ongoing happiness as nothing more than a fairy tale, wonderful to ponder but unattainable in practice. The individuals who discount or dismiss the possibility of creating total happiness will argue that bliss cannot be achieved when other human beings are suffering. How can true happiness be experienced while others go hungry and want for simple necessities? While there is so much rampant violence, hatred, and cruelty in the world? While there is so much prejudice, distrust, and suspicion? While the world has become too complex and jaded to even conceive of such happiness?

When people resign themselves to this limiting philosophy, they completely surrender their ability to make a significant, positive mark on the world by accomplishing their destiny. Instead, they pessimistically concentrate on their own day-to-day, bleary-eyed survival. And ironically, if someone considers the world such a negative place, and uses that hopelessness as an excuse not to make improvements in his *own* life, he certainly will not be able to contribute to the welfare of *others* to make the world a better place to live. Rather than mustering the initiative, strength, and courage to light a candle, he finds it easier to curse and wallow in the darkness.

I believe that's what many people unwittingly do to their lives. They narrowly focus on simply putting one foot in front of the other just to survive, living each day as miserably as the day before. Unfortunately, many people become "stuck" because they don't know what their talents and abilities are, and therefore have no idea about what objectives they could be achieving. They set no new goals and therefore have nothing to look forward to. Their philosophy is best stated as follows. "If I can just get going this morning, I'll be okay," "If I can just make it to lunch, I'll be okay," "If I can just make it to the end of the day, I'll be okay," "If I can just get back home to eat dinner, relax, and watch my television programs, I'll be okay," "If I can only make it to the weekend, I'll be okay," "If I can just meet my bills this month, I'll be okay."

If you have created this kind of life, you are not really living, but simply existing, as if you are marking time like a prisoner confined to a cell. Is each day of your life simply a clone of the day before?

For example, what do you have to look forward to *right now?* I'm not referring to the things you have *tentatively* planned for tomorrow, or next week, or next month, or next year, or five years from now. But *right now?*

How many fresh challenges are you accepting? What new people can you look forward to meeting? And where will you meet them? What additional skills are you building? Are you consistently feeling a sense of accomplishment? What greater risks are you taking? How will you structure tomorrow differently than today? What are you specifically doing to increase the level of financial abundance in your life beyond toiling in your current job? How are you creating a sense of romance in your life that is more inspiring than what you experienced today? How can you feel stimulated by each new day? How are you creating a sense of inner excitement about making your mark on the world? How can you feel the rewards of tangibly making a difference in someone else's life?

Can you even answer one of these questions? If you're like most people, you probably haven't a clue as to how you would respond, and may not have even considered all these dynamics. But don't be concerned! Try to avoid feeling depressed or frustrated over things that you have in your power to change. It's a tremendous waste of your precious time and energy. I pose these questions in order to inspire and motivate you to begin thinking of your life in different terms. *Your terms!*

All of the topics I just asked you to consider are dynamics of your spiritual destiny. You have it within your power to create a life not only filled with financial abundance, but also charged with the rush of success achieved by setting and reaching new goals, the heightened confidence and self-worth that results from meeting varied risks and challenges, the stimulation of a happy personal relationship, and the knowledge that you are here on earth to accomplish something meaningful that will have a positive impact on the lives of other people. Feeling this kind of unwavering purpose and utter fulfillment is the secret of happiness.

However, if you are surviving locked inside a prison of sameness and routine, you are not working toward your spiritual destiny, and the secret of happiness will always evade you as an impossible dream. All it takes to build a better life is the willingness to venture forth and escape the dreariness of your current existence by becoming aware of your destiny and mustering the initiative to achieve it. By doing so, you'll quickly erase the boredom, confusion, and lackluster routine of your life and begin a journey toward enlightenment that will lead directly toward secure and ongoing happiness. You *can* create an existence that yields emotional, spiritual, physical, and financial abundance, in which each day is profoundly different from the day before.

When I make these provocative statements, I'll always be specific with you. You won't be bombarded by a confusing avalanche of psychobabble or spiritual double-talk from me that causes you to ask, *what in the world is she talking about?* Let me explain, reader, that I'm a very pragmatic person. Whenever I tell you that something is possible, I promise I won't leave you confused or uncertain about *how* it is possible and exactly *what you have to do* to facilitate it. What I have learned from the spiritual beings with whom I've communicated is that building true happiness and peace on the earthly plane is definitely attainable, but *only* through the awareness and ongoing pursuit of accomplishing one's spiritual destiny.

Now that you understand how dramatically destiny effects your levels of happiness, achievement, and self-worth, you'll find it fascinating to consider the dynamics that make up *your* current destiny, or what I've referred to as the itinerary for your present earthly spiritual "vacation."

For instance, why did you decide to leave heaven to arrive on the earthly plane for your current lifetime? How is this historical period on earth pivotal in allowing you to accomplish your destiny? What does your "vehicle," or body, look like? How many spiritual destinations, or issues, are you attempting to explore? Why did you decide to be male or female? What is your life's work? Whom did you choose as companions? Which of your companions are soul mates? And when have you decided to leave the earthly "vacation" to return to your home in heaven?

As we continue to investigate spiritual destiny, you've already journeyed much farther than you probably realize toward greater understanding of your spiritual ''vacation'' here on earth. Let's now travel together down this path of self-awareness and explore the five guiding principles of spiritual destiny.

THREE

The Five Guiding Principles
of Spiritual Destiny

BEFORE ANY SPIRITUAL being leaves heaven for a ''vacation'' on the earthly plane, he must make a series of vital decisions that will chart his course and determine what he will be able to accomplish.

The decisions you make regarding your upcoming itinerary center on the issues you still have left to resolve, and are reached together with other people who are also choosing to return to the earthly plane and with whom you plan to interact. In addition, your plans take into account the existing level of enlightenment you earned from past earthly vacations, and what this enlightenment will allow you to accomplish as a life's work.

The course we chart will allow us to achieve as much as possible on our earthly journey, though we may be sidetracked from time to time by emotional upheavals, physical illness, and other obstacles.

One of the most provocative questions I'm asked during private channeling sessions concerns destiny's impact on our lives. Does destiny actually represent an inescapable series of preordained events that propel us inevitably toward certain people, places, or things? Or is it more accurately defined as a series of open-ended opportunities accomplished by an individual exercising free will?

Destiny can best be described as the *blueprint* of achievable goals we create for each earthly lifetime that form our purpose and direction.

While each spiritual goal we are meant to achieve is preordained from the moment of birth, the method we employ to accomplish each goal is open entirely to choice and free will.

Although the spiritual destiny that forms the depth and substance of an earthly life is predetermined by each individual before birth, how he goes about fulfilling it is up to him. Therefore, despite the fact that you have already specifically created your unique blueprint for this lifetime, the way in which you accomplish it is totally a matter of your own awareness, initiative, and perseverance. I refer to the decisions that form the blueprint, or spiritual agenda, for each earthly lifetime as the Five Guiding Principles of Spiritual Destiny.

The Five Guiding Principles of Spiritual Destiny include:

1. Life's Work
2. Issues to Resolve
3. Spiritual Contracts
4. Awareness of Past Lifetimes
5. Preventive Maintenance of the Physical Body

Each of the guiding principles represents a cornerstone in the foundation of your quality of life. It is only through accomplishing your spiritual agenda that you'll feel a sense of self-worth, direction, and purpose in your life, and become empowered enough to build relationships with people who will help create joy, peace, and contentment in your everyday existence.

Let's explore each of the Five Guiding Principles of Spiritual Destiny.

PRINCIPLE ONE: LIFE'S WORK

Without exception, everyone currently living on the earthly plane has a very specific kind of work to accomplish. Your life's work represents your purpose in this lifetime, or the mission you came to earth to fulfill.

Over the years, many of my clients have expressed profound embarrassment over the fact that they had always privately believed they had a life's work that involved making a substantial difference in other people's lives.

What I have learned through my channeled sessions is that *each and every one of us* travels to the earthly plane to make a difference in other people's lives. We are all reborn on earth to make a significant contribution to the welfare and spiritual progress of other human beings, and to hopefully leave something of importance behind when we decide to return to our home in heaven. If you have already sensed that *you* have an important kind of work to do, I applaud your awareness! If, however, you remain unconvinced about your ability to meaningfully contribute to the world and make your presence known, you simply have not awakened to the nature of your life's work.

One of the most astonishing revelations shared with me by my guardian angels is the fact that if a person on the earthly plane awakens to his purpose, and works to achieve it, he is guaranteed success, happiness, fulfillment, and abundance.

But how is this possible when so many people work

as hard as they do and never achieve success? Or any kind of happiness? What about people who have attained what appears to be the absolute pinnacle of achievement but who are bored and miserable? If success and abundance are guaranteed to all, why aren't more people happy and fulfilled?

The answer is simple: No matter how talented a person may be in a certain area, no matter how much money he makes, no matter how celebrated he is, no matter how many people may depend on him for their sustenance, he will never feel any sense of fulfillment if he has not discovered his life's work. No level of affluence or recognition can satisfy the hunger one feels inside his soul if he is not on his intended path.

By contrast, if you are already traveling the path to fulfilling your destiny, you needn't feel guilty about wanting a significant level of abundance that allows you to have a comfortable life.

As human beings, we help others move forward on their spiritual paths, but we must never forget that we also have a responsibility to ourselves, too. Therefore, when you become aware of your purpose, and keep striving to reach your goals, there is *nothing* standing in your path of success. If you work through adversity, sidestep unnecessary stumbling blocks, and keep focused on your goals, *you are a guaranteed success*! Consequently, if you have not reached a satisfying level of success in your life, you are not following the right path.

But how can you know exactly what your life's work really is? There are two wonderful sources of information available to you. First, I recommend that you look inward, and ask yourself this question. "If I had only one year left in my life and I could work in any occupation of my choosing—in which I would be assured of resounding success—what would I choose?"

By doing this, you're getting in touch with your soul,

and all the information recorded in its memory bank about your current life's work. You can be confident that you're accessing soul information when you sense a *passionate emotional feeling* in response to your question. If you don't feel any particular passion when you ask that question, perhaps you need to give yourself more time to become comfortable in accessing your feelings, particularly if you are more of a thinker than a feeler.

The second option open to you is asking your team of guardian angels about your life's work. From my experience, I can assure you that in no more than twenty minutes they can relay to you exactly what you planned for yourself as a purpose, how you can successfully move into your life's work, and how you can time the transition to make it as stress-free as possible. Having the ability to access such detailed and comprehensive information about your life's work is one of the best incentives you'll ever have to learn to channel!

You may be interested to learn that in most earthly lifetimes, you don't even have the opportunity to perform your life's purpose until you've reached your thirties or forties. Up to that time, you're fairly consumed by the business of resolving pesky issues that hamper your forward movement and chances of success. Of course, there are obvious exceptions. Shirley Temple started on the path of her very extraordinary purpose at the ripe old age of two!

However, because I recognize that retrieving information from the soul takes some practice, as does developing the ability to channel, I have created two detailed checklists that can help you, at a glance, determine whether you are currently in your life's work.

Key indications that you have found your life's work:

❑ You are currently happy and fulfilled by the work you are doing.

❑ You feel excited about getting back to work on Mondays.

❑ You're recharged and energized after you finish work each day.

❑ You have control over your structure, and can make decisions about your schedule. For the most part, you have the ability to determine when, where, and how you work.

❑ You have developed and embraced a leadership/ mentoring/teaching responsibility toward superiors, colleagues, and clients, which fuels you to inspire, motivate, and encourage their professional success.

❑ Frequent verbal and financial recognition is bestowed upon you for your consistent hard work.

❑ You regularly receive hard-earned promotions or you have started your own business.

❑ You're consistently stimulated by the work you do and the goals you are working toward. Each day is a little different from the day before.

❑ You feel an ongoing sense of freedom, achievement, and accomplishment, high levels of confidence, and positive self-esteem and self-worth.

❑ You are utilizing your strongest talents and abilities on the job, and often have the opportunity to develop heightened professional skills through successfully handling new challenges.

❑ You are inspired by a passion that continually widens the scope of your professional horizons.

❑ You have written goals that represent exactly

what you plan to achieve in the coming days, weeks, months, and years.

❏ Considering doing anything else seems totally disagreeable to you.

❏ If you have already started your own business, the thought of going back to work for someone else is repugnant and unacceptable. You love being the captain of your own ship and welcome entrepreneurial responsibilities.

Key indications that you are not doing your life's work:

❏ You are unhappy and unfulfilled by the work you are doing.

❏ In your heart, you dream about doing something else, possibly a type of work you fantasized about as a child.

❏ Family members, friends, colleagues, and even strangers comment, ''Have you ever thought about changing your job and doing such-and-such? You'd be so good at it!''

❏ You feel depressed at the thought of starting the work week. Sundays are particularly disheartening.

❏ You're drained and demoralized after you finish work each day, and find it harder and harder to recharge your batteries to feel better.

❏ You regularly overeat or consume junk food to emotionally comfort yourself.

❏ You check your watch consistently throughout

the work day, longing for breaks, lunch, quitting time, and the weekend.

❑ You feel frustrated because you have no control over your daily routine. Your boss or other colleagues dictate when, where, and how you work, with no input from you.

❑ You're tired of working for a demanding boss who isn't as productive, goal-oriented or intelligent as you are.

❑ You're resentful for not being verbally or financially recognized for your hard work, particularly in those instances when you rise above and beyond the call of duty.

❑ Although you perform well, are a good team player, and have shown dependability on the job, you feel an overwhelming sense of insecurity about losing your job.

❑ You're angry at being overlooked for promotions you've really earned.

❑ When you're at work, you find yourself looking around and wondering, *"What am I doing here? Why don't I feel comfortable or connected with anyone?"*

❑ You are bored by handling the very same tasks day after day, week after week, month after month, year after year.

❑ You have significant talents and abilities that you're not utilizing.

❑ You feel a profound sense of having outgrown your job and have nothing to look forward to in terms of transferring or being promoted within the company.

❑ You are not being financially compensated for the time, commitment, and experience you contribute daily.

❑ The thought of being in the same job a year from now makes you nauseous.

⤳ PRINCIPLE TWO: ISSUES TO RESOLVE ⤳

Along with performing your life's work, becoming aware of and resolving your outstanding issues will best help you improve your quality of life. Issues represent all the different forms of human experience on the earthly plane. An issue is a learning or growing experience that helps an individual evolve emotionally and spiritually. In heaven, each individual chooses which issues he will encounter, and therefore commit to resolve during his stay on earth. All the issues chosen represent the benchmark of what he intends to achieve for that entire lifetime.

You can easily recognize the issues you are currently working through by examining the apparent problems or patterns of dysfunction in your life. There are some issues that remain so painful for us that we carry them from lifetime to lifetime, attempting repeatedly to resolve them. Other issues can be easily worked through without much anxiety or suffering.

Moreover, like your life's work, the issues that you singled out for this particular lifetime are very different from those you have chosen for previous earthly ''vacations'' because the opportunities for spiritual growth shift and change according to what is happening on the planet historically.

Consider how singular periods in history have affected exactly *when* you've decided to return for a visit, and *what* you were hoping to accomplish in terms of your life's purpose and resolving outstanding issues.

Perhaps in a past lifetime you were a holistic healer in the lost continent of Atlantis; a celebrated performer in Shakespearean England; a victim of the Bubonic Plague; an artist during the Renaissance; a slave in nineteenth-century America; an American president, or a member of European royalty; an "untouchable" living in a Calcutta slum; one of Custer's soldiers at Little Big Horn; a shipping magnate during the Industrial Revolution; a passenger on the Titanic; a skilled flyer during World War I; a physician who developed a life-saving vaccine; or a Jewish mother of six young children living in Poland at the time of the Holocaust.

Unlike the delayed timing so often involved in accomplishing life's purpose, working on one's issues usually begins quite early in life. You may relate to the fact that many people who are on the earthly plane right now have chosen to start tackling distressing issues from very early childhood.

Being exposed to trauma at such a young age often has a shattering, scarring effect on children because they are completely vulnerable to the adult(s) in their household, helpless to make the transition out of the painful living environment. Children are the most defenseless participants in the hard work of dealing with issues— often not seen, heard, or considered until many years later when, in some cases, their own resulting dysfunction creates havoc and violent turmoil for others.

If your childhood was traumatic, remember you purposely planned that for yourself in order to learn from it. Those people who continually exposed you to their

*toxic dysfunction when you were a child have been your
very best teachers.*

You deliberately picked those troubled people (no dis-
respect to your family members) because you *expected*
them to behave just as they did at their existing levels
of enlightenment. Keep in mind that although you most
likely suffered many wounds, it was a very strong and
courageous decision on your part to plan something so
distressing, especially knowing that in your most for-
mative years you were to be utterly dependent on those
from whom you would experience the most adversity.
Think for a moment about all the spiritual wisdom and
maturity you gained from those impossible relationships,
and how you learned what *not to do* from them. And if
you've already learned everything you had intended,
you'll blessedly never be exposed to those issues again!

After I had been dating my husband Britt for several
months, we started to talk about our respective histories,
which included some painful memories of past relationships and the fact that we both came from dysfunctional
families. I described how my alcoholic father had bru-
talized my mother verbally and physically throughout
my childhood, and that the resulting long-term effects
were so devastating that I needed to spend more than a
year in therapy. His eyes filled with tears as he warmly
embraced me, and then he murmured, ''What a wonderful teacher he must have been. I can see why you
chose him as a father. You were very fortunate.''

Very fortunate? I thought Britt had gone completely
nuts! I was aghast that he said such a thing about a man
who had traumatized my entire family! What could I
possibly have *learned* from someone like him? From a
man I could never respect or depend on as a father?
Someone who rejected and abandoned me and my broth-
ers from the time I could remember because he was so
consumed with destroying my mother? I was in painful

therapy for over a year to heal and cleanse from these childhood wounds, and I *should be grateful to this man?*

Britt saw my shocked expression and before I could stutter a reply he explained softly, ''Don't you understand? *You chose him* as a father because you knew he would behave exactly as he did. You must have had some issues that you needed to tie up, and your father fit the bill perfectly. You're the person you are today partially because of that turmoil.''

That statement rang true to me, and I began to listen to him more rationally. I really started to see things in a totally different light. We discussed that because of the absence of my father's love, I had no feelings of security or consistency as a child. And due to my father's drinking and abusive behavior, I grew up in a war-zone environment characterized by ongoing financial hardships, fear of the sporadic beatings he gave my mother, and the awareness that at any time he might decide to make good on one of his frequent threats to kill her.

Britt helped me recognize that I didn't have to respect, admire, or even like someone who had a purpose in my life as a teacher. Spiritually speaking, it was my father's responsibility to me to act the way he did, and then it was my responsibility to myself to transcend the adversity and learn from it. So what was I able to learn from my father?

The early heartache of his neglect, rejection, and disinterest in me began the process of independence and empowerment that I am so proud of today. His abusive behavior toward my mother taught me about setting boundaries, as well as helping me understand the emotionally crippling effects of a low self-worth and self-esteem. In addition, as a result of moving beyond this difficult time, I was able to develop the determination to move through most of my adult transitions with little fear or hesitation.

Upon further reflection, I realized that I also learned what *not to do*. In my interactions with other people, particularly children, I always try to remember that every human being should be treated with dignity, respect, and consideration. Although my old wounds are healed and I've never been happier or more at peace, I can still vividly recall the terror of cowering from a parent gone berserk from the combination of anger and alcohol. The memory of those early years helps me to share a heartfelt sympathy and compassion for those who have similarly been mistreated.

Even in therapy I hadn't considered that my suffering could have been a precious learning experience and that my father was a valuable teacher. With his greater maturity and wisdom, Britt taught me that anything disturbing that happens in life can be turned into a positive learning experience as soon as I am ready to become a willing student.

In this regard, many of my clients have asked why life has to be so fraught with learning experiences. Why does it seem as if they are always starting over? Why, just as soon as they have cleared up one set of problems, are they bombarded by others? Why are they so driven to repeat the same patterns of self-destructive behavior in relationships over and over again? They ask why life isn't more satisfying or secure, like it seems for so many others.

What so many of us ask during the most gut-wrenching times of our lives is, "Why me? Why is it always me? What did I do to deserve this?"

Although there are a handful of enlightened souls who have already resolved all of their issues, rest assured that most people are still struggling with issues just like you are, no matter how flawless or successful their lives may appear from the outside. They may very well be working on different issues than you are, and the nature of what they're trudging through may seem much less arduous than yours at the present.

In spite of your spiritual enlightenment, it can sometimes be demoralizing to see other people create the kind of daily existence that you've only fantasized about, in which they've secured a blissful personal relationship, are raising well-adjusted children, have reached a pinnacle of professional accomplishment, have established financial independence, and maintain excellent health and fitness.

When one follows one's chosen destiny on the earthly plane, that quality of life is attainable. But when you're a witness to such fulfillment, but not currently enjoying that kind of existence, it can be extremely depressing— not because you begrudge the other person his quality of life, but because his success highlights everything *you* haven't yet achieved.

As a defense mechanism, it can cause us to self-destructively justify our own lack of initiative by thinking to ourselves, "Well, they have a special talent, so it's easier for them," or "Being born into an affluent family sure would solve a lot of problems," or "They're able to be successful because they don't have to contend with insecurity, or fear of failure like I do because they didn't have my childhood!" or "He/she had success so early, they'll never know what a real struggle is!"

These uncomfortable feelings can provide you with an incentive to work toward a better life. If you can replace those "If only it were me" negative patterns of thought with the more positive "If he/she can do it, I can do it" type of philosophy, you'll develop a powerful new ability to move forward and create the quality of life *you* most desire.

At the same time we're feeling sorry for ourselves, it's amazing how superior we can act toward friends and family members who are struggling with issues we've already resolved. For example, have you ever found yourself thinking any of the following?

"What is taking him so long to see the problem? Is he a nincompoop? I'm going to help by giving him my advice!" or "Why is she so self-destructive? Why can't she just muster up the gumption and give up the addiction? I'm going to give her the name of my psychologist!" or "How can she allow herself to be treated that way? Why doesn't she stand up for herself? If that happened to me, I'd give him a piece of my mind! And I'm going to tell her so!"

If you've actually *said* anything like this, especially when no one asked for your opinion, you're trying to teach someone who has not yet indicated that they are willing to be your student. I realize that you're only trying to help someone in a trying situation, but to an individual who really isn't ready to move, it may feel as if you're dragging them forward kicking and screaming! We've all had that experience, and it certainly isn't pleasant at the time, especially if *you're* the one on the receiving end. A client of mine describes the situation like this: "It's like trying to teach a pig to fly. You won't get anywhere, and it makes the pig very annoyed."

Do you realize those very same family members, friends, and acquaintances who are still grappling with the issues you've worked through, see *your life* as simple, secure, and so much less difficult than theirs?

Have you ever had someone say in all sincerity, "Well, you just don't *understand*. Life has been so *easy* for you. You've *never* had problems like *mine*."

What they're doing is insinuating that you've never had to struggle or worry, and that perhaps things have simply been *handed* to you. If you've been the recipient (target?) of such a remark, you were probably dumbfounded and possibly angry. When such statements have been made to me, I've discovered that it's pointless to argue. I try to consider that perhaps I've worked through some issues that they haven't, and my life could very well seem, from the outside, much less complicated than theirs.

I also believe that if you can rely on your sense of humor in the process of resolving issues, the ability to laugh at yourself, as well as appreciate the hilarious irony in life, it will certainly help make your "vacation" on earth so much more tolerable and pleasant.

Unfortunately, when it involves a learning experience, rarely do we learn anything without significant adversity, which often makes us feel as if we've been hit over the head with a twenty-pound iron skillet. What's more, some of us have to be whacked over the head several times before we figure things out, which makes us pretty bruised in the process. Even worse, sometimes we continue to get hit over the head and still remain clueless about what's going on.

I have to admit I'm the poster girl for people who need to be reminded of an issue several times before they finally get it resolved. If you're like me, rest assured that bruises heal, and you'll have gained a tremendous amount of hard-won maturity and enlightenment in the process. Believe it or not, those of us who take a little while longer to learn have a distinct advantage—when we finally recognize an issue and learn from it—boy, have we learned!

Consequently, if you keep repeating the same patterns of derailing problems from job to job, or from relationship to relationship, you must ask yourself, "What am I missing? What is the lesson I am supposed to be learning here?"

Become aware that we draw to us the learning experiences we need at that time. There are no accidents in the universe. Everything that happens has occurred for a specific reason, and at a time that will ultimately be most beneficial for all involved.

In regard to the troublesome people in your life, understand that each stressful relationship has a specific purpose involving the resolution of shared issues. Concentrate on the people in your life with whom you have dissension. What are you supposed to be learning from them? What, if anything, are *you* contributing to the dysfunction? I know that question might make you bristle, and I certainly recognize that we all have certain malfunctioning relationships in which we are *not* responsible for the discord.

However, when it's appropriate, try to avoid the self-destructive and self-righteous habit of blaming others for *all* the disharmony that exists, because if you fail to recognize *your* accountability in the spiritual equation, the universe will continue to provide the same frying-pan-over-the-head learning experiences until you do. And as you've probably discovered the hard way, as I have, the learning experiences that focus on the same issues get tougher and more serious as time goes on.

How can you determine how thoroughly you're addressing your issues? I'm going to share a wonderful, insightful exercise with you that has been recommended to a number of my clients by their guardian angels.

Sit down with a notebook and pen to perform what the angels refer to as ''taking stock.'' The process of taking stock is an extremely valuable investment of your time and energy because it will help you understand what you've been doing with your spiritual and emotional energies, and how much you've actually grown, even if it seems to you as if you haven't been accomplishing anything at all.

Set aside several hours and find a comfortable spot where you won't be disturbed. What you're going to do is look back over the last ten to twelve years of your life. Arbitrarily pick a starting point that reflects a difficult situation that you experienced. It could be a lingering injury or illness, a hurtful relationship, an awful job, or a memorable financial hardship. Just make brief notes about each episode in a sentence or two, and continue to recall anxiety-filled trials and tribulations that readily come to mind until you reach your life at the present. You'll probably end up with quite a list! Then, entry by entry, go back over your list and ask yourself how you would handle each dilemma if it were to occur *today*. This is the fun part!

Although it might initially sound like a depressing exercise, it is actually one of the most emotionally reassuring tasks you'll ever perform! I promise that once you start examining how you would respond to the exact same set of problems today, you'll be amazed at how differently you'd react. You might even find yourself chuckling at imagining how the others involved in these past dysfunctions might be affected by your newfound assertiveness and maturity. You'll learn how wisely you've been investing your time and energies and how much you have actually learned from the accumulation of all those events.

You'll likely discover upon reflection that you're a totally different person now than you were five years ago. This encouraging realization will allow you to acknowledge that as long as you work on your issues, you'll always continue to grow spiritually and evolve into a very different person enjoying a far better quality of life several years from now!

You can "take stock" as often as you like. It's an extremely important exercise because without it, it's difficult to objectively determine how successfully you've been moving forward. To that end, no matter how distracting or disheartening you find your issues now, try to develop a positive attitude in regard to working them through.

All the issues you will encounter during this earthly vacation are the learning experiences you intentionally chose while mapping your current spiritual agenda because they represent the issues you knew could be resolved in this lifetime.

If you're beginning to wonder why you should even address issues from the past that will very likely be hurtful, or labor-intensive and time-consuming to resolve, as long-standing issues are certain to be, consider the alternative.

Ignoring or avoiding long-standing issues will ensure that your quality of relationships, level of professional achievement, and financial abundance will remain exactly where they are *right now*. Are you satisfied enough with your current levels of fulfillment and security to imagine yourself in the very same position one year from now? Five years from now? Ten years from now? That's exactly the life you'll be creating if you procrastinate. The scary thing about issues is that they'll always be there waiting for you, no matter where you go, what you do, or with whom you interact.

Although I resolved the childhood issues I had with my father by the time I was in my early twenties, I was to be bombarded with a series of very different issues in a dysfunctional marriage several years later.

Besides being in the chaotic relationship, I felt clueless about my purpose and direction. Out of ignorance, I fervently denied that I had any responsibility for the state of my life, and instead I blamed everybody else. I deluded myself by thinking, "I'm a good person. I would never intentionally hurt anyone. Don't I often put other people's feelings before my own? I haven't done anything to deserve this unhappiness. Why are all the people in my life so impossible?"

As the years went by, I became even more miserable. When I finally realized that the people in my life weren't going to do anything to change their dysfunctional behavior, I came to understand that I would never have their cooperation to make improvements in my life. That acknowledgment hit me like a ton of bricks. If they weren't interested in improving our relationship, then I was trapped where I was.

It occurred to me that perhaps I really didn't *need* their cooperation to be able to change my life. Maybe I couldn't enhance any of my existing relationships, but I could certainly work on *myself*. After all, just because my father and I were not in contact and he didn't get involved in my therapy, I was still able to resolve all the issues connected with *him*.

At that moment of awakening, I understood *accountability*. I decided to explore *my* responsibility for the problems in my life, and how I had been unknowingly perpetuating them by denying accountability. When I started slowly working on them, one by one, I couldn't believe what I discovered.

All the anger, frustration, insecurity, and unhappiness I created by avoiding and denying my issues had been, in truth, much harder to deal with than the *actual process of working them through*! Never mind all the precious time and energy I wasted! You can take my word for this. Remember, I was the poster girl for having to learn everything the hard way!

Little by little, I could feel my life improving. On a daily basis, the heavy weight of dysfunction I carried for so long was remarkably dissipating, and I knew a lightness of spirit that I wanted to share with everyone. I came to an awareness of what it means to *release the struggle*.

So what happened to the people with whom I had the

dysfunctional relationships? What was their response to my work on self?

My newfound enthusiasm for becoming emotionally healthy and free from dysfunction was incredibly threatening to some people, and served as an inspiration for others to start their own work. But I learned that it didn't really *matter* what the other people in my life decided to do. Ultimately, they are in control of what they decide to do with their lives and the quality of life they want to build. I couldn't nag, push, cry, cajole, coerce, encourage, or coldly withdraw from someone in my life who was choosing to remain where they were in terms of their issues.

I discovered that such behavior was presumptuous, judgmental, and controlling of me, in spite of my good intentions. I was resolving issues and wanted to help everyone else do the same. But people are either ready to resolve issues or they're not. As with deciding to embark on a program of diet and exercise, the motivation has to come from inside of them.

Those people in your life who are ready to work on their issues will show positive interest in the work you are doing. They will want you to share what you're learning and discovering, and will encourage and support your progress. If they're not ready or interested in working on issues, they'll likely be cold, negative, threatened, angry, or sarcastic about the work you're doing.

Again, remember that is a decision they are making about their *own* lives, which they have a right to do. But don't let anyone else make you feel guilty, or manipulate you into derailing your progress because they are intimidated or threatened that you're going to evolve into a different person. Isn't that the whole purpose in doing the work in the first place?

We all have a responsibility to self to discover exactly what issues we still have to contend with, and get them resolved as quickly as possible so we may move on to a future that is happier and more secure than the present. To that end, I strongly recommend that if you've been attempting to work through an issue for some time, and have been continually unsuccessful, you might want to consider visiting a good therapist who can help speed up your progress.

The following list represents contemporary issues that are most frequently addressed in my channeling sessions by both male and female clients. You might peruse the list and ask yourself if any of the entries pertain to you at this time.

In addition, it's interesting to note that although men and women can be very dissimilar in their philosophies and how they respond to others, there are surprising similarities in some of the issues we are all attempting to resolve.

Common Issues Affecting Women	*Common Issues Affecting Men*
Developing an awareness of gifts, talents, abilities	Developing an awareness of gifts, talents, abilities
Desire to control others	Desire to control others
Independence	Becoming less left-brained or anal
Empowerment	Anger
Self-reliance	Commitment phobias
Self-worth, self-esteem	Self-worth, self-esteem
Assertiveness	Emotional openness

Fear of abandonment	Fear of abandonment
Confrontation (argumentative)	Confrontation (emotional)
Setting boundaries with others	Setting boundaries with others
Fear of success	Fear of failure
Being accepted for who she is	Being accepted for who he is
Becoming a victim of verbal and physical abuse	Becoming a victim of verbal and physical abuse
Addiction to alcohol, drugs, food, sex	Addiction to alcohol, drugs, food, sex
Monogamy	Monogamy
Denial	Denial
Loneliness	Loneliness
Rejection	Rejection
Physical illness	Physical illness
Manipulation	Manipulation
Procrastination	Procrastination
Ability to take risks	Ability to take risks
Sexual abuse	Sexual abuse
Loss (death of loved one)	Loss (death of loved one)

ᴚ PRINCIPLE THREE: SPIRITUAL CONTRACTS ᴇ

A spiritual contract is a binding agreement, or commitment, reached on the heavenly plane between two or more parties who plan to interact with each other during an upcoming earthly lifetime.

Have you ever wondered about the purpose behind all your important relationships? Have you considered that each and every family member, friend, colleague, and acquaintance has entered your life for a very specific reason? All of the significant people in your life have a commitment to fulfill with you, as you do with them. You may even have a spiritual contract with someone who is meant to pass through your life in mere minutes, hours, days, or weeks!

There are basically two different types of human interactions that exist on the earthly plane. First, there are the *learning-experience* types of relationships in which two people come together to learn from each other. Second, there are the *soul-mate* types of relationships in which two people come together to provide unconditional love, peace, and contentment for one another.

In a learning-experience relationship, you connect with another person to address a particular issue, or group of issues, until the issue is explored or in the best case scenario, completely resolved. Learning-experience relationships may emerge quite pleasantly and without incident, but in time *always* erupt into various levels of confusion, miscommunication, loneliness, frustration, and anger. In some cases, these spiritually important relationships begin with immediate dysfunction and turmoil, and continue to boil explosively.

There are other instances in which your learning experiences are much less dramatic and the relationship is not abusive or hurtful, but instead has become unmistakably stale and sour. At this juncture, you may feel bored to tears and quite anxious to move on so that you may start "living" again. Toward the end of a learning experience, at the time when you have spiritually accomplished everything you were supposed to from the relationship, you are likely to lament: "My husband [or sister/mother/best friend/business colleague, etc.] is never going to grow and try to work through our issues. Things will never change and I realize now that I'm not being true to myself if I remain in this relationship."

The relevance of your learning-experience relationships is that they are intended to provide a sense of *balance* for you to learn from. The people with whom you interact in these types of relationships are all either working through exactly the same issues you are, or issues that represent the complete opposite end of the spectrum. Remember that the whole purpose of an earthly vacation is to be a sort of spiritual boot camp for you to accomplish the dynamics of your particular destiny and return to the heavenly plane a much more mature and enlightened being.

For example, perhaps when you were mapping out this current "vacation," the person who agreed to be your sister committed to helping you develop your existing levels of assertiveness and setting boundaries because she needed your help with her issue of control.

It very well could be that the person who agreed to be your best friend committed to helping you address your issues of denial and confrontation by being physically intimate with your husband because she needed your assistance with her issue of monogamy.

Possibly, the person who agreed to be your spouse committed to helping you resolve your issues of independence, empowerment, and self-esteem because he needed your support with his issues of anger and abuse.

Likewise, the person who agreed to be your daughter committed to helping you work through your issue of procrastination because she needed your guidance with her issue of impatience.

You can easily identify a learning-experience relationship. It is one that causes your heart to ache and your mind to agonize and your body to become ill from continued exposure to a particular person.

This is the reason that so many of your relationships may be teeming with friction, turmoil, stress, and miscommunication. As learning experiences, they are supposed to be! Each difficult relationship is actually very precious to you in terms of what impact it can have on your enlightenment. Moreover, the length of time you devote to working through the dysfunction is completely up to you.

Although you are morally bound by any spiritual contract you make with another being to interact for the purpose of resolving issues, you may remove yourself from the relationship at such a time as when you determine your part of the commitment has been fulfilled.

When you were planning the dynamics of your current earthly vacation and deliberating prospective learning-experience relationships, your decisions included not only what specific purpose the interaction would have, but also the time frame you allotted to accomplish the work with that individual. Learning-experience relationships are rarely meant to last a lifetime, no matter if the other individual is a spouse, parent, adult child, sibling, best friend, or business partner.

As you may have already discovered, when you encounter the person with whom you are to have a learning experience, the issues you both planned to address are quickly activated. Whether it happens immediately upon first glance, or months into the relationship, you'll feel a conspicuous disharmony between the two of you that is distracting and stressful whenever there is contact.

When the problems first arise, you'll be making your life so much easier if you take a moment to figure out the purpose of the turmoil and exactly what you are supposed to learn from it. Until we build the awareness of why the learning experience exists, we are condemned to repeat the very same patterns of draining, upsetting dysfunction.

In this regard, many people have particular family members or colleagues who can't get along and who always have friction between them. Those individuals keep having the very same arguments about the same issues, trying to pull others into the fray.

Isn't it amazing that certain issues never get resolved because people don't take the responsibility to come to terms with what they themselves are contributing to the problem? So much precious time is completely wasted in arguing over who is *right* and who is *wrong*. Deliberating about who is right and who is wrong and expecting others to take sides is completely nonsensical. Being right is not the issue at all. If the relationship is truly meant to be a learning experience, *both* parties have something to learn, as well as something to teach.

Working through issues is actually much easier than most people make it out to be. I believe the hardest problems we encounter are those we needlessly create by avoiding, ignoring, or denying our learning experiences when they first erupt. Some people have such a miserable quality of life because they keep repeating the same patterns of adversity and hardship.

Perhaps the biggest roadblock they create for themselves in terms of successfully learning on the earthly plane is insisting on always being right and having all the answers to everything. This stubbornness destroys any chance they might have had to resolve their issues.

Now let's assume that you are a spiritually responsible

person and you are indeed successfully identifying all of the relationships you have planned as learning experiences. Let's also assume that you recognize the purpose behind your difficult relationships and you are working to resolve those issues.

By contrast, what happens when the other person with whom you are sharing the learning experience doesn't want to grow? What happens if he doesn't want to take responsibility for his side of the equation and refuses to work with you to resolve issues and create a better relationship?

At times, you have probably found yourself in this truly unfortunate situation. When this occurs, many of us somehow turn into a type of teacher that wants to "help" the student even if it means dragging him forward kicking and screaming. After all, aren't we *right* in our estimation of where the other person is going *wrong*? Can't we clearly define in what way the relationship is currently lacking and how it could potentially evolve if only the other person would shape up?

Coming into this kind of clarity is an integral part of successfully interacting in a learning-experience relationship. However, you can't magically instill this hard-won awareness inside a stubborn or reluctant partner no matter how hard you try.

If you find yourself in a learning-experience relationship with an unwilling partner, there is light at the end of the tunnel. You can still do *your* work and benefit from the relationship *exactly as you had planned*, without the cooperation of the other person involved.

Although this situation isn't ideal, your only option is to accept the fact that your learning-experience partner has decided to stay where he is in terms of enlightenment. Therefore, you must consider moving on to do the work you originally intended. The only other alternative is to remain in the dysfunctional relationship for as long as you or your partner draw breath in this lifetime.

Figuratively speaking, this scenario is akin to hitting a bump on the highway during your vacation and getting a flat tire. Your traveling companion decides that it is simply too hard to fix the tire and he prefers to sit by the side of the road for the rest of the vacation. At the same time, you understand that it is also within your power to fix the flat. Are you going to allow your companion to derail the rest of *your* vacation? Are you going to fail to fix the tire simply because your companion has decided that *he* prefers to sit where *he* is? What about the wonderful vacation plans that *you've* worked so hard on for this lifetime? It's very possible that if you choose to be true to yourself and fix the flat, you'll end up driving off to continue your vacation without your companion. But you'd certainly offer him the opportunity to help you fix the flat tire so that the two of you could continue the trip as planned. It would be entirely his *choice* not to participate, and so it would be his *choice* to remain where he is. He has the right to decide how productively he is going to spend *his* vacation, just as you have the right to determine what you will do with *yours*.

The faster you let go of your disappointment in your partner's unwillingness to move forward, the faster you'll be working through those issues and crossing the threshold into a better quality of life. Accepting your partner's decision also means that you refrain from thinking, "But maybe the relationship can change. I know I can help if I try hard enough." By adopting the "I can change him even if he has no desire to change" kind of attitude, you'll end up resentfully sitting by the side of the road next to your indifferent companion wondering what has happened to your beautiful vacation plans.

Instead of complaining about how uncaring, unfeeling, insensitive, lazy, and procrastinating your partner is, muster the gumption to fix that flat tire yourself and be on your way! I know from personal experience that it certainly isn't easy to let go of an important relationship, no matter if the learning-experience partner is a parent, spouse, adult child, best friend, sibling, in-law, or business colleague.

You can't take responsibility for the decisions made by another adult or make them move forward if they don't want to.

Although you certainly don't have to agree with them, you have no option but to *accept* another adult's choices, even if those choices completely derail what the two of you were supposed to accomplish together. But be reassured that you *do* have complete power and authority over what *you* choose to do with *your* own life, regardless of the decisions made by others, and regardless of what *they think* you should be doing. Happily, the situation works both ways!

The second type of human interaction that exists on the earthly plane are *soul-mate* relationships, in which two people come together who have a true affinity for one another previously established in past lifetimes.

In a soul-mate relationship, you connect with another person to support, encourage, inspire, love, and motivate each other to reach your full potential. There are no troublesome issues between you to resolve, although one or the other partner may still be engaged in the process of addressing issues with other people outside the relationship.

Contrary to popular belief, a soul-mate relationship is not necessarily always romantic, and does not invariably involve sexual intimacy. However, a true benchmark of a soul-mate interaction is that it does inspire a profound spiritual and emotional intimacy between partners. Soul mates may include significant others, siblings, parents, children, friends, acquaintances, and colleagues. The soul-mate relationship most often ignites when both participants recognize an immediate affinity or familiarity with one another unlike anything they've previously encountered. From the start, both people feel they really "know" each other, and can discern their partner's most positive attributes.

In contrast to a learning-experience relationship, soul mates grow closer and more bonded as time goes on. The soul-mate relationship is one characterized by mutual trust, respect, affection, harmony, and inner peace. In a soul-mate relationship, we joyously realize, "It's absolutely incredible that I get along so well with another human being! Someone finally understands and accepts me!" A soul mate can help us perceive the very best of who we are, while providing ongoing inspiration and encouragement to continue spiritual growth. There can be no better or truer traveling companion for your earthly "vacation" than a soul mate who knows who you are and appreciates where you are going.

You can easily identify a soul-mate relationship. It is one that causes your heart to bloom, your mind to soar and your body to become energized from continued exposure to a particular person.

It is also very common for soul mates to share a telepathic communication in which they can read each other's minds, finish each other's sentences, or speak volumes with a simple glance. This intuitive familiarity has been developed as a result of sharing numerous past lifetimes in close, trustworthy relationships.

Moreover, each earthly lifetime is unique in terms of how we plan soul-mate interaction. There are some "vacations" we plan devoid of any soul-mate encounters, and in other earthly lifetimes, we may enjoy numerous soul-mate relationships. Having the opportunity to share any part of one's life with a soul mate is a true gift, and serves to remarkably balance and soften the learning-experience type of relationships. The extraordinary union between soul mates is the only kind of interaction between partners that is eternal and everlasting, prevailing as successfully on the difficult journeys to the earthly plane as it does in heaven.

☜ PRINCIPLE FOUR: AWARENESS OF PAST LIFETIMES ☞

Developing an awareness of what you have achieved in past lifetimes is of paramount importance in becoming confident in your ability to successfully travel the current spiritual path you have chosen.

This awareness will dramatically enhance your self-worth and self-esteem because you'll understand that you're actually a composite of each and every past lifetime you've experienced. Therefore, if you decide to explore your past earthly lives, you'll appreciate how and why you chose all of the specific dynamics of your *current* spiritual destiny, and how it is possible to accomplish your goals.

Many lifetimes ago, you crossed over the threshold to begin the journey of the spiritual destiny now in progress. Each consecutive lifetime forges another bead on your string of enlightenment. Your string of beads represents what you have already achieved. This string, which describes your soul's memory bank, acts as a tether to past lifetimes while continuing to weave the fabric of your current and future lives on earth.

Accordingly, the life's path you have chosen is connected to all the journeys you have traveled before. Your ongoing destiny actually represents a continuum of relationships, careers, and issues you've already successfully encountered. If you have chosen a life's work that involves healing, you have very likely performed as a healer in previous lifetimes. If you are meant to be a writer in this lifetime, you were very possibly a writer during an earlier earthly vacation. As you become aware of your spiritual history, you will dramatically enhance your ability to resolve prevailing issues, as well as inspire greater levels of professional and personal confidence. When you fully realize that in a past incarnation you've *already been successful* in your particular life's work and in manifesting a loving relationship, the heightened self-awareness will effectively fuel your courage and determination to launch into a new, more electrifying sense of purpose. You'll understand that the pursuit of your destiny is supported and fortified by your soul's *existing* skills and abilities, and the spiritual agenda you are now striving to fulfill is simply an encore to what has been previously accomplished.

In this regard, let's assume a friend has asked you to make him some of your special chocolate-chip cookies. When you think about the task of baking cookies, you remain calm and confident knowing that you've made them before, and they have turned out beautifully. The thought of baking the chocolate chip cookies is not intimidating and does not fill you with concern. You're confident that success in baking the cookies is a foregone conclusion. Do you see where I'm going with this analogy?

You'll begin to realize that your spiritual agenda for this lifetime is not as daunting as you suspected, and truly achievable because you've reached similar goals before.

If you happen to be a skeptic about reincarnation because of your beliefs, or because you attach greater weight to matters that can be proven empirically, I fully respect your position. However, you may be inclined to change your philosophies after exploring this chapter!

As a skeptic, if you acknowledge that the earthly plane presents the opportunity for people to grow into more mature and enlightened beings through experiencing various types of adversity, then how can you explain the fact that some individuals return to heaven while still in infancy or in early childhood? If reincarnation does not exist, and we are meant to have only one lifetime on earth, how can those babies possibly gain the wisdom and enlightenment necessary for their spiritual evolution in such a limited time frame?

I believe the existence of multiple lives is also tangibly evident in the enigmatic and staggering resources of child prodigies, whose mystifying genius has been recorded throughout history.

For example, in 1761, Wolfgang Amadeus Mozart began work as a serious composer at age four. In 1814, Carl Witte, already an accomplished mathematician, earned a doctorate in philosophy from the University of Giessen, Germany, at the age of twelve. In the late nineteenth century, Pablo Picasso began to draw before he could speak, and while still in infancy, his first attempts to communicate resulted in a babylike request for a pencil. And despite the fact that the Great Depression in the 1930s proved financially cataclysmic for many Americans who found themselves out of work, Shirley Temple began her triumphant career in films as a professional actress, singer, and dancer before the age of three.

How can such brilliance in the arts and sciences suddenly blossom in an individual so unworldly and immature? Have you ever considered how a child who has had little, if any, apparent mentoring could have within him an *existing* level of extraordinary talent and expertise? If you are a skeptic, how would you account for the exceptional capacities in a prodigy, particularly if you believe that we are all accorded only *one single lifetime* on the earthly plane? If indeed we only visit the earthly plane for a single vacation, how and when did the child study or train to develop his genius? If you believe that the heavenly plane is singly responsible for inspiring and supporting the development of such genius, and that we all come from heaven, then why don't a greater number of little children exhibit prodigal tendencies?

Have you ever questioned where *your* childhood gifts and talents came from? Do you remember feeling a comfortable expertise with something the very first time you tried it, as if the ability was second nature to you? Although your endowments may not have resulted in worldwide acclaim, perhaps you were a budding artist, musician, writer, athlete, mechanic, or perhaps you were gifted with languages, computers, or numbers, or found that you were the center of attention and could make others laugh.

The talents and abilities you were able to access from early childhood represent past-life experience that has been previously recorded in your soul's memory bank.

Similarly, throughout your current life, you'll continue to access soul memories that will allow you to feel comfortable with certain projects or challenges that you're attempting for the first time.

By contrast, if like most people, you suffer from some type of puzzling fear, anxiety, or phobia, it very likely took shape in past lifetimes as a trauma so frightening or hurtful that it remains in your consciousness today. Try to recall the people, places, or things that caused you to feel mystifying apprehension or despair when you were a child. Then take into account your present fears or hesitations that have no discernible origin. You're in very good company if you suffer unexplained feelings of foreboding in connection with certain people, places, or events.

Given the fact that you've never had a difficult encounter with water, why do you have a fear of drowning? If you've never been traumatized in a confined environment, then why are you claustrophobic? If you've never witnessed a plane crash, why are you afraid to fly? If you've never been ridiculed or attacked by an angry mob, then why are you terrified of speaking before a group? Perhaps you have a fear of snakes, or fire, or a certain illness, or being violated, or abandoned. Maybe you're afraid of being alone. While you may not realize the source of your fears, you do know that you are not paranoid, and you have not deliberately created these fears to intentionally feel uncomfortable. That would be ridiculous, wouldn't it?

Through the process of channeling, I have discovered that almost without exception, an individual's seemingly irrational fears or phobias are actually the haunting memories of trauma experienced in past lifetimes.

During many of my private sessions, I've had the opportunity to explore past lifetimes for clients who wish to learn how their prior circumstances may still be affecting them today. As a result of channeling for thousands of people, I have come to believe that we are *all* affected by what we've experienced in past lives. Although I've often channeled for clients about past lifetimes that were joyous and quite satisfying, I have also "seen" past lives that have been extremely traumatic and disturbing.

But the possibility of learning about trauma in a past life should not deter you from learning more about your wealth of spiritual experience. In fact, shedding light on past life difficulties can allow you to discover the *cause* of your current fears, anxieties, and issues. Once you learn about the *cause*, or root, of a particular obstacle or difficulty, you are able to let go of its *symptoms*. To successfully resolve issues, we must always dig until we expose the root of a specific problem. It is as if you had a particularly stubborn weed at the heart of a beautiful garden. If you were to only focus on the part of the weed you could see and cut it down to the soil, it would quickly grow back and be just as unsightly as it was before. But if you dig until you reach its root and remove the core of the weed, it would be gone forever.

Similarly, there are times when we must dig into a past life to get at the root of an issue. It is true that recalling a previous existence in which you've had unfortunate encounters is upsetting, but remember—*you're reviewing a past life that you've already completed*. We all have a fear of the unknown. But if you muster the courage to review difficult past lives, you'll release all the emotional baggage you have carried away from them. To further clarify, I'd like to share a fascinating past-life channeling session that revealed the root of a very significant present-day problem.

On one memorable afternoon, a woman came to see me to get help with a condition that was beginning to threaten her sanity. Since early childhood, she had an overwhelming fear of water.

Ironically, she had grown up in a lakeside community whose residents frequently participated in water sports including boating, skiing, swimming, and fishing. She was the only member of her athletic family who feared any body of water bigger than a bathtub.

Her family and friends did everything to "help" her resolve this phobia by way of nagging, teasing, cajoling, and sometimes actually forcing her into the water, which only made her more terrified. No one could comprehend how this phobia started, or why she couldn't just "forget" or "get over" her anxiety. Eventually her family assumed that she would grow out of the phobia, as if it were an allergy or an adolescent skin disorder.

As time went on and she matured, the fear became more pronounced. She couldn't even look at a small body of water without hyperventilating. At this point, she decided to try an alternative method of solving her problem and soon found herself sitting across the desk from me. During her first session, we discovered what was at the root of her problem. It was indeed so unspeakable, that like most traumas, it had transcended time and space to remain as vivid a fear for her at the present as it was when it was actually occurring.

I channeled that in her last lifetime, as a young girl, she had been a passenger on an ill-fated passenger ship and had experienced a hideous death by drowning. She perished while locked in the bowels of the massive ship, amid the blinding chaos generated by women and children screaming in anguish and praying for mercy as they were swallowed by the rising, icy waters.

As the session continued, my client began to cry, clearly "remembering" what had transpired so long ago that had created such a fear inside of her. She finally understood why she had always been so intimidated by water! The process of recounting what had happened opened her soul's memory bank and allowed her to courageously acknowledge the pain and suffering she endured. In doing so, she was able to quickly let it go. Through tears and choked laughter, she declared that she suddenly felt lighter, as if a great weight had been lifted from her heart. We had successfully dug to the root of her phobia, which enabled her to forever erase the symptom of her tremendous fear of water.

By contrast, the phenomenon of reincarnation can also cause us to have very *positive* recollections. For instance, have you ever sensed familiarity with a place you're visiting for the first time? Or with a particular task you're initially attempting? This intuitive recognition of an unknown, but yet familiar entity is referred to as déjà vu, which is the emergence of past-lifetime information from the soul's memory bank. The recognition often occurs as a short burst of "Twilight Zone" type of awareness that makes us realize, "I've been here before. I don't understand how, but this place [or activity] is totally familiar to me."

You may also experience déjà vu when you first encounter a person with whom you've shared past lives. This explains the paradox of meeting someone for the first time and immediately recognizing them as familiar to you.

Upon meeting someone with whom you've shared positive past-life encounters, you'll experience a warm, cozy feeling and a real desire to spend time together with the intention of "catching up." Almost immediately after reuniting with a kindred spirit, the soul's knee-jerk reaction to comforting familiarity will inspire trust, affection, and respect to resonate within you, and soon you'll be finishing each other's sentences!

Equally significant is the converging energies of two individuals who have had difficult relationships in past lifetimes. The soul's knee-jerk reaction to once again encountering such disharmony will serve to inspire caution, suspicion, and dislike from the moment you meet. When you encounter someone whom you immediately dislike, it is possible that your soul is warning you about a dysfunctional relationship you've already encountered with this person in a previous life.

Developing the existing levels of your intuition will allow you greater recognition of past-life people, places, and events.

When I first met my husband Britt, I immediately sensed a warm familiarity that deepened into a spiritual bond that I had never experienced before. We both quickly recognized that we had been together in previous incarnations and that we had a romantic purpose with one another in our current lifetime. Britt was eager to move the relationship forward, and when he proposed marriage several months after we met, I joyfully accepted. I felt as if I had always known him, and I knew in the deepest part of my being that he was a soul mate who was meant to be a profound part of my destiny. With keen anticipation, we began to plan our wedding.

At the same time, the closer we became, the more I acknowledged a fear of him leaving me and never returning because of an unexpected accident, or even worse, an act of foul play! These premonitions were especially worrisome due to the fact that I was a psychic channel who was regularly accustomed to intuiting information about impending danger. From experience, I knew I wasn't being paranoid.

Although I channeled on the situation and my angels reassured me that no such event would take place, I remained frightened every time Britt left the house. There was a small but unmistakable voice inside me that kept insisting that I would suffer tremendously in connection with my relationship. This irrational, gnawing anxiety grew stronger with each passing day. Of course, I was hesitant to disclose this premonition to Britt, thinking that it would scare the daylights out of him. But as the voice persisted, I felt I needed his support. When I shared what was happening, he understood completely. With his usual insight, Britt suggested that the problem might be erupting from a previous incarnation the two of us had shared and he recommended we search for answers in a past-life regression. I must admit that although I do this for clients on a daily basis, it never occurred to me that my own unexplainable fears had their roots in past-life experiences!

Rather than channeling for the two of us and explaining the events to Britt as I "saw" them taking place, we decided to share the experience and go under hypnosis together to begin what we assumed would be a lengthy foray into past lifetimes. We visited a hypnotherapist, and in a little more than two hours, we had all the answers we were looking for.

The first hour shed light on a French lifetime we shared in 1452. We had been married for ten years and had three small children. We owned a small farm. Britt suddenly developed clairvoyant powers and spent many hours writing what he psychically "saw." As his wife, I was terrified of the reaction the church would have if they learned he had paranormal abilities. To further develop his enlightenment, Britt decided to make a pilgrimage to Italy. He remained there for one year. Upon his return to France, he became ill with the plague. In spite of my frantic efforts to save him, he died in my arms. After his death, church officials demanded to search our home as a result of local gossip about Britt's clairvoyance. When they discovered his journals, the officials condemned his writing as proof of witchery, and burned me and our three children at the stake in the town square.

Next, we were transported to a lifetime in Russia. The year was 1865. Britt was a man called Alexander Ivonovich. I was his wife, and my name was Olga. We worked together as scholars, traveling to small villages throughout Russia teaching philosophy, music, literature, foreign languages, and the sciences. We lived in a blue frame house, with shutters the color of fresh cream. In the spring and summer there were always colorful flowers around the cottage because Alexander loved to garden. Being more practical, I thought spending time in the garden was foolish because flowers died so quickly, but my husband was fond of saying, "My darling Olga, everything worthwhile dies, except ideas."

Alexander and I were becoming known throughout Russia as teachers, openly speaking about peace and freedom. We were warned by the czar's soldiers to stop what they considered treasonous. We continued to speak out because we wanted to leave something of benefit behind that would remain after we were gone.

The czar's soldiers came to our cottage one night. They turned over furniture. They destroyed what we had worked so hard to build. We pleaded with them to stop. The soldiers forced Alexander outside. I screamed for him, but two of the czar's men held me back.

In no more than few moments, the soldiers roughly pushed me aside and left our home. I ran outside after them. It was getting dark. As they rode away I could hear them laughing.

I saw Alexander on the ground. He had been stabbed. There was blood everywhere. I rushed to him, sobbing, and knelt down to cradle him in my arms. And he said, "I don't want to leave you—"

I begged him not to die. His blood was soaking my dress. My husband looked up into my eyes, and died clinging to me. I did not want to live without my dear Alexander. I left him to search for one of the wooden stakes he had carved to border the flower garden. When I found it, I laid down beside him and prayed for my salvation. And then I gathered all my strength and drove the stake into my chest. My soul left my body and I quickly joined Alexander in heaven.

In that past-life regression, I learned why I was so frightened about losing Britt in some kind of tragic accident. When I "recalled" what had transpired in two of our previous incarnations, I'm surprised I hadn't felt compelled to chain him safely to the living room couch! As a result of our regression, I was able to dig into the root of my concerns and comfortably let them go.

❧ PRINCIPLE FIVE: PREVENTIVE MAINTENANCE ❧ OF THE PHYSICAL BODY

Your physical body is the housing that you've chosen to provide the earthly support system for your soul.

Knowing how to effectively maintain the health and safety of your body is fundamental in achieving your spiritual destiny. If your body's well-being is compromised, it could impede or completely derail your spiritual forward movement. In the event your earthly support system suffers a total shutdown, the entire "vacation" comes to an end, and your soul has no option but to return back to its home in heaven.

Each of the Five Guiding Principles of Spiritual Destiny fit together like cogs in a wheel. The wheel is meant to carry you smoothly through your earthly vacation, gracefully rolling toward all of the spiritual destinations you plan to reach.

The cogs in your wheel are represented by elements including your life's work, issues to be resolved, spiritual contracts, awareness of past lifetimes, and the preventive maintenance of your physical body. If there are unsettling conditions in your life that are not being addressed, your wheel will break down.

All the cogs need to be in sound working order for the wheel to move forward. Maintaining the integrity of your wheel and its forward movement is very simple: You must become aware of all the dynamics of your spiritual destiny and consistently work to achieve them.

In this regard, if you spend an inordinate amount of time hesitating or refusing to meet spiritual challenges, the cog that represents that particular dynamic of your destiny pops out of the wheel frame and any additional forward movement is impossible. Unfortunately, when one cog pops out of the wheel frame and we don't immediately address the situation, other cogs begin to come loose and the wheel becomes increasingly difficult to repair. This is essentially how you create periods in your life when problems begin to escalate one right after the other and you feel as if your sanity is being tested. In this instance we're actually creating much more difficulty in our lives than we were *meant to experience*. Learning to immediately respond to a difficulty when it first arises may actually *prevent* other cogs from popping out of the wheel frame, thereby limiting the number of issues you're forced to deal with at any one time.

Thankfully, it's not difficult to recognize the signs of a breakdown. For example, are you stuck in an unfulfilling relationship? Do you feel stymied in finding your romantic soul mate? Are you trapped in a dead-end job? Are you defeated because your level of income can't properly sustain you? Do you lack the physical energy to resolve one or all of these situations?

Sitting by the side of the road watching other people's wheels roll by with purposeful momentum is very demoralizing, but you'll remain there until you act as your own mechanic and accomplish three spiritual tasks. First, you must determine whether any breakdowns currently exist. Briefly examine all the different facets of your life. How happy are you? In which areas are you experiencing insecurity, discord, or unhappiness? The portions of your life that immediately come to mind represent breakdowns.

Next, you must decide what you need to do about the breakdown. Third, you must follow through with the necessary *action*. Simply having purposeful intentions will not fix your wheel. You must follow through and *act. Until you act, you will remain stuck exactly where you are right now*. It doesn't matter if there are some facets of your life that *do* appear sufficiently satisfying. When one cog has popped out of alignment, it stops all other forward movement until the problem is corrected.

Despite the fact that you may know exactly where your setback has occurred, you might not know how to successfully repair the problem. *You must fix your own breakdown*. There is no other mechanic who can solve your problems.

At the time of a breakdown, your soul comes to the rescue. Each of us has a built-in user's manual inside our soul that will provide assistance should we encounter an unexpected complication. The user's manual includes all the vital information essential to your spiritual agenda, namely the destinations you are scheduled to reach in this lifetime, and the time frames in which you planned to reach each destination.

What's more, the manual that allows you to be your own mechanic is yours alone. It does not lend itself to other people's breakdowns, and so efforts to "help" friends or loved ones with their breakdowns will always be unsuccessful. That's also the reason why you must not wait to be rescued from your current life situation by another person. If you waste time waiting for help, you'll spend your life miserably sitting by the side of the road.

Many of my clients have expressed a frustration in finding themselves in a recurring dilemma. Although they realize just where they've broken down, they don't understand how to access their soul's user's manual to successfully *fix* the problem. When they request intuitive information, their angels always reply that they *already know what to do*, but they hesitate out of fear, emotional and physical exhaustion, laziness, and/or procrastination. Most always, we understand how to react to a breakdown, but we are unwilling to take the action necessary to start moving forward again.

To that end, consider the areas in your life where you've previously acknowledged you have a breakdown. Then be honest—in your heart, you already recognize what you have to do to fix the problem, don't you? How do you know? Because your soul, or user's manual, starts flooding you with important "fix-it" information through your emotions the moment there is an impending breakdown.

For instance, when you experience a breakdown in a relationship, your soul intuitively suggests one or more of the following *actions*.

- Working toward better communication
- Seeking outside therapy
- Temporarily or permanently removing yourself from the negative situation

When you experience a breakdown in your career or financial resources, your soul intuitively suggests one or more of the following *actions*.

- Pay off existing bills
- Become more conservative with spending habits
- Discontinue spending on credit
- Decrease monthly living expenses
- Seek a new job within or outside of your company
- Explore a new field of work
- Start your own business

When you experience a breakdown in your physical health, your soul intuitively suggests one or more of the following *actions*.

- Improve your eating habits
- Begin an exercise program
- Take vitamins
- Seek help from the conservative medical community
- Seek help from holistic practitioners
- Remove yourself from continuing personal and/or professional stress
- If you're suffering from a fatal disease, prepare for your transition back to the heavenly plane

When you experience a breakdown in your spiritual momentum, your soul intuitively suggests one or more of the following *actions*.

- Learn to channel directly with your angels
- Read spiritual books to expand your horizons
- Attend spiritual lectures and classes given in your area
- Make new friends with others who are actively on their spiritual journey
- Visit a spiritually-based, nondenominational place of worship

Do these answers appear too simple? Our lives on the earthly plane were always intended to be simple! We merely overcomplicate our lives by *delaying work on simple repairs*. Initially, the repairs on the wheel could be handled rather easily. But as we dismiss or ignore the repairs, the situation continues to worsen.

For example, what would happen if you had a serious toothache? Could the condition simply get better on its own? Probably not, and if you fail to address the predicament, it will probably deteriorate further. Wouldn't it be much easier to fix the problem when it first appeared?

Imagine you've just been contacted by the Internal Revenue Service about an unexpected financial complication. It is highly unlikely that this problem will magically disappear. As the days tick by, the dilemma becomes increasingly complex and worrisome because you're accruing penalties and interest. This is exactly what you're doing to yourself when you fail to fix a spiritual breakdown when it's first occurring. You're literally accumulating emotional, spiritual, mental, and physical penalties that alarmingly snowball until they threaten a collapse of your entire quality of your life.

The *physical* penalties that accrue can be particularly devastating. You can actually destroy the good health and longevity you originally planned for this lifetime by neglecting to respond to spiritual breakdowns when they first occur.

Long-term emotional, spiritual, and mental breakdowns can bankrupt the vitality of your life support system and completely cripple what was to be good health and longevity.

Prior to each rebirth on the earthly plane, you have specific choices to make regarding your physical body, including the dynamics of your health and well-being; your longevity; your gender; the color of your skin, hair, and eyes; your height; and your body type.

In my seminars, I am frequently asked why some people are plagued with illnesses or disabilities, while others enjoy vibrant good health. There are three variables that dictate the state of each person's physical body.

First, you may have deliberately chosen to experience an illness or injury as a particular *issue,* which when encountered, will help build upon your existing foundation of maturity and enlightenment. When a health condition arises because you purposely planned it as one of your issues, you either meant to recover and live many more years on the earthly plane, or by contrast, you have chosen to contend with a fatal illness that will ultimately force you to return to the heavenly plane long before you reach old age. A physical incapacity may help an individual develop greater inner-strength and self-reliance, as well as build his or her compassion for others who are less fortunate.

In 1994, my mother had a very serious injury to her right leg and was forced to occupy a wheelchair for almost two years while she underwent a series of painful surgeries that she hoped would restore her mobility. While she was in the wheelchair, we were constantly amazed at the number of people who would rudely stare and conspicuously move away from her when we'd go out on errands, as if she were contaminated. Even worse, because I needed both hands to push her wheelchair, I was often forced to depend on others to open doors for us in public places. People would simply watch my struggle to push her while trying to open a heavy door at the same time, without ever walking a few feet to come to our aid. I would always have to *ask* people for their help before they would reluctantly respond.

Our greatest source of frustration was that we'd often see vehicles parked in the wheelchair-designated parking spaces without disabled tags, completely preventing us access to our destinations. On the occasions when I would actually confront someone who had parked illegally, they would excuse their behavior with a dismissive, "But there was no other parking available!" or "I was only running in for a minute!" It was continually astonishing to my mother and me how thoughtless people could be, never realizing how limiting and difficult it is for those who are disabled and wheelchair-bound.

Following her sixth surgery, my mother is now thankfully back on her feet. Because of what we learned, we remain extremely sympathetic to those less fortunate and less mobile. We are now eager to render aid to someone physically disabled because we know exactly what they are going through and we consider it a privilege to have the opportunity, through some small act, to make their life a little bit easier.

The second variable that dictates the health of the physical body involves *past lifetime ailments and injuries* that continue to emerge and affect current vitality. When a client comes to see me and complains of an ongoing illness, I begin my search for answers by exploring that person's past lifetimes. It is fascinating to discover that sporadic colds or flu may be haunting reminders of bubonic plague, pneumonia, consumption, or perhaps having frozen to death in a past life. A persistent neck ache might be traced to a previous lifetime in which a person was beheaded, strangled, or hanged.

The third variable that affects the state of an individual's health and well-being involves *self-destructive behavior* that can actually alter what was to be a healthful physical destiny. When an individual fails to respond to intuitive warnings of impending danger, or fails to react to spiritual breakdowns in a timely manner, it can often cause illness, injury, or in some cases, premature death. Therefore, a person's destiny can be altered to such a degree that it irrevocably changes how he will make his transition back to the heavenly plane.

While it may be virtually impossible to extend your time on the earthly plane beyond what you had planned, it is possible that you could engage in behavior that would dramatically shorten your earthly visit.

Let's speculate that you planned to die peacefully in your sleep at the age of ninety-three. But let's also consider the fact that you have an abusive husband who has repeatedly battered you emotionally and/or physically. This would be a very good example of a spiritual breakdown. If you chose to do nothing in response, you could return back to heaven long before you anticipated because of his volatile behavior.

How could another individual's behavior so dramatically affect the state of your health and well-being? In addition to the obvious life-threatening ramifications of physical battering, the human body is terribly affected by emotional and mental turmoil. Exposure to continual stress at work or at home will eventually cause your body to exhibit signs that it isn't completely ''well.''

If you currently feel sick, it is unlikely that you suffer from paranoia or hypochondriac tendencies. There is probably something wrong, and your body is trying to warn you about an impending or existing illness with symptoms that are meant to get your attention.

Akin to the wealth of information you receive from your soul, your physical body regularly communicates about the state of its health. We tend to take the health and well-being of our physical bodies for granted, often neglecting to follow a healthy lifestyle. When the body announces "I'm sick!" through symptoms of nausea, discomfort, pain, or just a general state of malaise, we often refuse to listen to what the body is trying to tell us, and are instead frustrated at the inconvenience of the symptoms. How many times have you reacted to illness or injury by announcing, "But I'm too busy to be sick!" or "I just can't afford a sprained ankle right now!"

Once the physical body begins to suffer from exposure to repeated mental and emotional anxiety, it will often react by creating disease or injuries that will distance you from the source of the turmoil.

Have you ever pulled a muscle, broken a bone, endured headaches, waves of queasiness, or an eruption of an unsightly skin rash during particularly hectic periods of your life? Have you ever suffered flu-related symptoms during or just following a enormously stressful time at work? Most people can directly relate disruptions of physical well-being to the existing levels of stress in their lives. When this occurs, we often react by thinking, "I just let myself get run down because I've been so busy. I'd sure like to spend a few days concentrating on getting better, rather than on all the problems I'm facing in my daily routine."

Does this mean that there is no such thing as a virus, or bacteria, or other disease-causing agent that will affect you? Of course not. However, when your physical body starts to manifest disease on a *regular basis*, even though your symptoms may be as minor as a nasty lingering cold, constipation, headaches, or repeated bouts of the flu, it is trying to tell you something! Your body is trying to tell you that if you *remain* in the stressful environment, the emotional and mental strain that you regularly suffer will *eventually* create a much more serious physical condition. It could take years before a terminal disease emerges, but if a potentially fatal illness is not meant to be a part of this earthly vacation for you, why risk it—especially if stress-related health problems are already in progress? Undoubtedly, your soul has already been nagging at you to remove yourself from the troublesome environment before it's too late.

It is equally important to discuss how protecting your physical safety is yet another dynamic in maintaining the longevity that you planned for this lifetime.

Are you haphazard in regard to personal safety habits? Do you keep the doors and windows of your home and car unlocked? Do you recklessly walk or jog in unsecured areas at night? Do you open your door to anyone who knocks? Do you agree to indiscriminate rendezvous with strangers you've just met in an environment that makes you vulnerable? Do you ignore threatening phone calls, unannounced visits to home or work, strange notes or letters, stalking, uninvited touching, or offhand but inappropriate remarks? Do you return home late at night and risk a lone walk through an unguarded parking lot? Most important, do you put yourself in physical jeopardy because you dismiss intuitive feelings that warn of impending danger?

To ensure the departure date you originally chose to go back to the heavenly plane, you must take full responsibility for your health and safety while on your earthly vacation. In practicing preventive maintenance, you must fuel your body with healthy foods, exercise, get enough rest, and refrain from drug use, smoking, and alcohol consumption. You must also remember to employ your common sense and natural intuitiveness to help you derail any unnecessary exposure to physical violence.

Until I began channeling, I believed that a person's cause of death and their age at death was absolutely predetermined and therefore was unalterable destiny. However, I was surprised to discover how easy it is for an individual to shorten the length of his earthly visit by sabotaging his physical health and safety.

Many spiritual beings I have communicated with have expressed tremendous sadness and frustration because human beings have failed to heed their intuitive warnings and unintentionally cut their earthly lives short.

Pay attention to what others have discovered and learn from their mistakes. Safeguard your physical health and safety, and you'll ensure that your time on earth will be stimulating, healthy, productive, and as lengthy as possible.

At this time on the earthly plane, we have a lot of choices in our health care. If a health condition arises, we may seek out physicians and traditional medical practices—hospitals, surgery, pharmaceuticals, and emerging technologies that can cure and rehabilitate patients in the throes of even the most serious of illnesses or injuries.

Many individuals are now, however, becoming partners in their own health care by practicing *preventive* health maintenance. In the event that illness or injury does occur, an increasing number of people are exploring alternative methods of recovery that include holistic healers, acupuncture, chiropractic medicine, colonics, lymphatic drainage, chelation therapy, massage, vitamin therapy, reflexology, aromatherapy, meditation, and even sea-salt baths.

I strongly suggest that you let your intuition direct you to the healing methods most appropriate for you. If you are unsure about alternative methods of healing and recovery, you might consider visiting a bookstore or library to take advantage of the wealth of research conducted in all the above-mentioned therapies. To find an experienced practitioner in your area, get a reference from someone you trust, or contact a holistic clinic. Metaphysical bookstores are also a great resource in terms of seeking a referral.

Now that you have developed an understanding of the Five Guiding Principles of Spiritual Destiny, and how destiny is established by accomplishing a spiritual agenda, you are prepared to learn exactly how you plan your agenda before embarking on a new earthly lifetime.

FOUR

❧❦

Choosing Your Spiritual Destiny

IS THERE ANYTHING more exciting than planning a vacation? The sense of joyful anticipation can be overwhelming, especially during periods when you're feeling burned out because of a stale home life or stressful career. Just daydreaming about the trip can be exhilarating and can recharge your batteries!

Spiritual beings living on the heavenly plane experience the same feelings of exhilaration when they contemplate a return to earth for another vacation. Although in heaven you certainly won't be suffering from an emotionally empty personal life or a mediocre career, you *will* be yearning for the opportunity to build spiritual growth.

As spiritual beings, we are not satisfied to rest upon the laurels of previous earthly achievement. Building spiritual enlightenment can only happen on the earthly plane because an individual is challenged with adversity that forces him to grow. Unlike planning a trip that is restful, fun, or pampering, when a spiritual being decides to make the miraculous journey back to earth, he intentionally schedules an arduous series of hardships and ordeals that represent his unresolved issues, and his life's work.

The heavenly plane and the earthly plane offer two very different and unique spheres of existence. We live on the heavenly plane as spiritual beings driven by the soul, and we live on the earthly plane as human beings driven by a combination of heart, mind, body, and soul. Each time we return to the earthly plane we are reborn into a physical body that houses not only the soul, which governs our spiritual awareness, but also the heart, which is intended to be an emotional compass that helps us make decisions and take risks; and the mind, which tempers the spontaneity, passion, and emotional capacities of both the heart and soul.

While in heaven, we remain acutely aware of what is happening on the earthly plane because it is the only realm where a soul may earn greater levels of wisdom, enlightenment, and maturity. Any soul living in heaven may choose to make the journey back to earth whenever he wishes, and most souls are extremely eager to repeatedly make the trip.

While we are toiling and trudging on the earthly plane, we are observed with unwavering vigilance by an army of guardian angels that guide the human souls entrusted to them. Other spiritual beings, including numerous ''deceased'' friends and family members, often assist angels by watching over loved ones on the earthly plane, providing them with support and encouragement.

As we begin to discuss how a spiritual being makes his transition back to the earthly plane, you may remain unconvinced that any soul would ever want to leave the peaceful, harmonious, and joyous security of heaven for *any* reason. Why would anyone in their right mind decide to journey away from such a magnificent existence to one in which they deliberately plan to experience mental turmoil, emotional melodrama, physical pain, and frightening financial chaos?

To those of us currently living in that environment, such a decision seems unfathomable. But to those living on the heavenly plane, the opportunity to return to earth is met with tremendous enthusiasm and anticipation, as it is the greatest means by which one can unselfishly contribute to the welfare of others, and by doing so, elevate one's own soul to a higher level of enlightenment.

Elevating one's soul sounds like a very altruistic and burdensome objective, doesn't it? It *is* a rigorous and labor-intensive task, but that is exactly what makes each of our earthly vacations worth the effort. Meeting and overcoming adversity is how we earn a sense of achievement that makes life on earth worth living.

Your enlightenment has been achieved by triumphing over countless challenges and misfortunes in thousands of past lifetimes on the earthly plane. The ghastly trials and tribulations all happen for a specific reason. They are meant to be valuable learning experiences. Those learning experiences, or issues, represent all the different forms of human understanding and awareness. Your soul progresses spiritually depending on how quickly and consistently you recognize and resolve issues on the earthly plane. Once you've resolved all of your issues, you no longer have to return to earth for a spiritual vacation, and you may remain in heaven for all eternity.

How do you know when you've resolved all of your issues? Remember that on the heavenly plane, you have a complete awareness of what you've already accomplished and what you have left to do. Until all issues are completely resolved, each soul yearns to further expand his existing levels of spiritual awareness by embarking on yet another earthly incarnation.

You may be saying to yourself, "Well, when I get back to heaven, if there really is such a place, I'm never going to leave! I'm never going to choose to come back to this !@&#! place again!"

Experiencing an earthly vacation myself at the moment, I can certainly understand why you'd have that reaction. However, when we're on the heavenly plane, we feel remarkably different about earthly vacations. We human beings are often incredibly short-sighted about *future* goals and desires. We always assume that the way we feel *right now* is the way we'll *always* feel.

For example, if you were to ask your six-year-old son to give a kiss to a female relative, you might hear him contemptuously decline by announcing, "I don't care if it is her birthday! I'm not gonna kiss her! I'm never gonna want to kiss a girl!" Your son's passionate remark would probably make you smile, because you'd assume that one day in the not too distant future he will develop a completely different attitude toward the female gender.

Typically, we human beings routinely react with surprise and negativity to almost *anything* that is beyond our current focus or imaginings. I frequently encounter this kind of resistance during private channeling sessions.

For instance, my clients often ask me about the nature of their life's work. Because many of us remain ignorant about our spiritual agenda, it's very common for us to be clueless about our purpose, too. It's fascinating to me that when I channel specific information about the dynamics of a person's life's work, the person often resists the information and responds with disbelief. Why does this occur? I believe that a person may discount what he hears about his own staggering potential because he is afraid and intimidated when he learns that he can reach unlimited success in an endeavor *outside of his current pursuits.* It's commonplace to disbelieve or deny anything that does not currently ring true to us, or exist on our *immediate* to-do list.

On a daily basis, I hear clients passionately refute what their angels are trying to communicate about their life's work. "*Me*, write? But that's *impossible*! I can't even *spell*!" and "Open my *own business*? But that's *impossible*! I've never even thought of going into management!" and "Outside *sales*? But that's *impossible*! I've never *sold* anything in my *life*!" and "An *artist*? Me? But that's *impossible*! I haven't painted since I was a kid!" and "Become a consultant and *public speaker*? But that's *impossible*! I've never even *thought* of speaking in front of a group!"

Believe me, I can relate to this resistance, because I had the same reaction when my angel John first described what I was supposed to be doing in the future. My response to him was, "Are you *crazy*? How can I channel for *other people*? I've never done that before!" At a later date, when he told me a big part of my life's work would be speaking in front of groups, I assumed he had gone completely nutty. With my natural shyness, I never thought that was possible. In time, however, I did give him a chance to explain that I had chosen public speaking as part of my purpose to help me work through issues that centered around being bashful and insecure.

We unknowingly limit ourselves and short-circuit awareness and success by refusing to look beyond our current philosophies and immediate plans. One of the most important ingredients to success and accomplishment on the earthly plane is simply *never say never*!

Spiritual beings look upon upcoming earthly lifetimes as fantastic, challenging spiritual adventures, in which they have the opportunity to become an intrepid pioneer voyaging to an unpredictable, volatile planet where any nature of things may occur to test their mettle, determination, and courage.

The dawning of each new day on the earthly plane presents a fresh opportunity to lift oneself out of unhappiness and dysfunction to start building a sturdy foundation of security and contentment.

Once you have decided to embark on another journey to the earthly plane, you must make a number of decisions to help you accomplish as much as possible during your "vacation." In fact, even if you plan to remain on the earthly plane for more than one hundred years, it is still considered a short stay according to heavenly time frames.

While some of the decisions about your new life you make autonomously, others are made between you and fellow spiritual beings who are also in the planning stages of their next earthly lifetimes. Through this exhaustive process you create the framework of your spiritual destiny, which includes the who, what, when, where, and why of your upcoming vacation.

You must begin by choosing your life's work, issues to be resolved, spiritual contracts to be honored, healthfulness of the physical body during your stay, and longevity, which determines the length of your vacation. Once this framework has been developed, other significant arrangements follow, including the selection of your gender, parents, siblings, friends, spouse(s), your physical appearance, the time and place of your birth, race, religion at time of birth, socioeconomic background, and geographic location at birth.

We also have the opportunity to elect to be born singly, or as part of a multiple birth. In addition, if we decide to be adopted because the experience will help us resolve outstanding issues, then we must pick not only our birth parents, but adoptive parents as well. Together these choices form the cornerstone of your very unique and individual spiritual destiny.

Although you make commitments with other spiritual beings as to how you plan to interact with them, all of the final arrangements you make regarding each of your earthly lifetimes are made by you alone. No other heavenly being, including God, the great legion of guardian angels, or your ''deceased'' family or friends pressures you or dictates how you should plan your earthly existence. You have the total freedom to designate what you plan to accomplish in each earthly incarnation, and this autonomy underscores the accountability you feel once you return to heaven and reflect upon how successfully you've fulfilled your earthly agenda.

The main reasons we keep returning to the earthly plane are to resolve outstanding issues, and to fulfill a particular purpose that will ultimately have a positive impact on the lives of other people. Therefore, the two most important decisions we make when planning a future earthly incarnation involve the issues we opt to address and the life's work we intend to accomplish. It is certainly gratifying and reassuring to learn that no one makes these decisions for us, and that we have the complete freedom on the heavenly plane to strategize about all the specific variables that will determine the personality and direction of our entire lifetime.

In a place where miracles are the rule instead of the exception, and nothing is impossible, it is truly remarkable to note that perhaps the most inspiring moment for any heavenly being is the time his earthly vacation plans are on the drawing board and he once again is becoming the architect of his destiny.

To begin the exciting process of setting an earthly lifetime in motion, a spiritual being must make a number of key decisions.

CHOOSING YOUR ISSUES

Without doubt, the most time and effort you spend deliberating about your future life is invested in choosing your issues. This is your first and foremost consideration, and all the other dynamics of your life will be structured around the issues you intend to resolve.

To make this very important decision, a spiritual being carefully reviews the issues he has already successfully worked through in previous incarnations on the earthly plane. Next, he examines those issues he still has left to resolve. Some of them will require a great deal of work because they haven't yet been addressed, while others will require a simple tying up of loose ends. Usually a spiritual being is inclined to combine a series of issues in various stages of completion as a sort of balance, to help him build well-rounded enlightenment. However, when a spiritual being anticipates extreme or unusual hardship in connection with certain issues, he may plan an entire lifetime around those few learning experiences to allow himself the best advantage to triumph over these adversities.

As a spiritual being weighs his options about his next earthly lifetime, he remains exceptionally optimistic about how much he will be able to achieve. This is the reason that, at times, you may feel so overwhelmed by issues. While you were orchestrating this current lifetime, you deliberately planned to encounter a wide variety of problems because they represented what was left to complete on your spiritual to-do list. Therefore, any issues that you encounter and decide not to address will remain outstanding, and you can rest assured that they will most definitely surface in a future earthly vacation.

Interestingly, those remarkable beings who have already resolved all of their issues can still arrange to return to the earthly plane to help others who remain struggling. In those situations, a spiritual being would still make all the other plans for his destiny, including a life's work, gender, birthplace, and spiritual contracts, but would have the opportunity to live his life free and clear of the pain and anxiety so often caused by earthly issues. If you're wondering if anyone actually ever reaches that level of enlightenment, I can assure you that it is indeed possible. A number of my clients have already worked through all of their issues, and now look forward to investing more of their time and energy in helping others.

Once you have settled upon the issues you will encounter, it is time for you to make another vital decision. You must pick a life's work that will not only add to your existing levels of maturity and wisdom, but at the same time, contribute to other people's quality of life.

🐦 CHOOSING A LIFE'S WORK 🐦

Choosing a life's work is a thrilling enterprise! This process involves exploring your existing gifts, talents, and abilities developed in numerous past lives, and strategically determining how you will integrate those abilities with the issues you have just established.

In previous earthly lives, you may have been a brilliant artist, but in your next incarnation, you may instead elect to become a pilot, an athlete, a physician, or a manufacturing entrepreneur. We are often inclined to build new skills in areas that have been previously unexplored to further strengthen the foundation of experience from which we are working. Sometimes we feel disposed to continue working toward the very same goals we set for earlier incarnations, which explains the occurrences of unschooled genius in small children.

Reaching an awareness of your life's work and striving to meet your true potential is a guaranteed path of success that will allow you to make the very most of your life.

After you have established your issues and life's work, you now must choose a physical body and the length of time you deem appropriate for this particular earthly vacation.

CHOOSING YOUR PHYSICAL HEALTH AND LONGEVITY

Each lifetime is very different in terms of your body's healthfulness and longevity. During some of your earthly lives, you will enjoy perfect health and will return to heaven only after successfully reaching old age. In others, a difficult health issue, such as cancer, may force you to return to heaven while still very young.

The issues and life's work you have chosen will dictate your health and longevity. If you have decided upon a very challenging career, the physical body must carry out its responsibility of sustaining the soul, heart, and mind to allow you the freedom to achieve your spiritual agenda.

At times, a serious physical illness or injury will actually inspire an individual to move forward into his life's work. For example, an illness such as cancer can act as a catalyst to motivate an individual to do something he never would have considered otherwise, such as become a healthcare activist, an author, or a public speaker discussing what he has learned about his illness. Remember that there is no such thing as a coincidence. If you or a loved one has suffered from a serious physical illness or impairment, take note that it happened for a very specific and important reason. Typically, the condition is meant to refocus an individual's life in a brand new, much more satisfying direction.

Besides determining health and longevity, you also can choose exactly how you want to look in your next lifetime by establishing your eye, skin, and hair color.

The final choices of height and body type will be reached during the next stage of decision-making as you consider gender.

✒ CHOOSING YOUR GENDER ✒

In each of us there is a measure of both male and female qualities. Male qualities reflect the mental and physical centers of the body, and include endowments such as assertiveness, dynamic risk-taking, physical strength, logical reasoning, unemotional problem solving, confidence, and leadership abilities. Female qualities reflect the emotional and spiritual centers of the body, and include endowments such as verbal communication skills, intuitive awareness, sensitivity, creativeness, emotional problem-solving, understanding, and supportiveness.

During private sessions, some clients have asked why they have gravitated toward a gay lifestyle. Although they are completely comfortable with their sexual orientation, they remain curious as to the spiritual reason behind their choice. When asked, their angels explained that they intentionally made the choice to be gay in order to achieve greater understanding of a particular gender. An individual who is gay accomplishes several lifetimes worth of work in a single earthly vacation, because of the continual personal exposure to members of the same gender.

For instance, women who engage in a lesbian lifestyle

have had a higher number of previous lives as a male, and therefore wished to build their awareness of what it is to be female by devoting an entire lifetime to interacting with other women. Accordingly, men who engage in a gay lifestyle have had numerous past incarnations as a female, and wished to build their awareness of what it is to be male by devoting an entire lifetime to interacting with other men.

As a mature, enlightened individual you probably recognize a combination of both genders within you because you have been both male and female in previous incarnations. We all opt to switch genders in various lifetimes in order to develop a balance inside our soul that will serve to increase the levels of our existing enlightenment.

The *time* in which you decide to return to the earthly plane is an additional factor in determining gender. For example, if you settled upon the issue of building leadership skills, and a life's work as president of the United States, you'd have to plan your gender accordingly to allow the opportunity to achieve what you desired. If leadership and presidency had been your agenda, and you desired to attain your goals by the turn of the twentieth century, you certainly wouldn't have been inclined to return to the earthly plane as a *woman* because at that time, women who were American citizens didn't even have the right to vote! Yet, ironically, you could have returned to the earthly plane hundreds of years before, as a woman, to work on the issue of leadership as Queen Elizabeth I, who aggressively led England to its recognition as a world power.

〜 CHOOSING THE MOMENT OF YOUR BIRTH 🜂

After determining your gender, you must arrange the exact moment of your birth. Not only do you deliberately single out the most advantageous astrological birth sign, but you also determine the day and time to reenter the earthly plane. This ability to establish one's exact moment of birth explains why some births take place prematurely, while other pregnancies continue interminably until labor must be induced.

Each particular astrological birth sign represents certain strengths and weaknesses, because precise planetary alignment at any given second will reflect and determine the personality traits and tendencies of those born during that time.

This variation in the year, date, and time of birth accounts for the fact that people sharing the same astrological sign may be very different from one another. If you know two people born on the same day, in the same year, and they are still remarkably different from one another, it's because of a disparity in the levels of enlightenment they brought into this lifetime with them.

In addition to birth sign, there are a myriad of other astrological variables that represent the position of various planets at the moment of your birth that also contribute to the entirety of your personality.

For instance, in this current lifetime, I desired to be a female, and to work through issues of independence, empowerment, and self-reliance. My astrological sign is Libra, which among other things, represents all forms of partnerships. I deliberately chose Libra, the sign of partnerships, because it dovetails beautifully with my challenge to go it alone, and realize that my life is just as complete with or without a partner. I also chose to be born at a time when there were several important planets in the sign of Aries, which represents no-nonsense, dynamic forward movement and spontaneity. These inborn Aries traits are perfectly suited for my ongoing challenge of working through issues of impatience, and learning to accept the fact that my schedule is often far too ambitious. I regularly lament, "Why hasn't such and such happened yet? I've waited long enough!" Before my recent marriage, I often had this Aries-influenced telephone conversation with my mother, who is, by the way, a nurturing Cancer.

MOM: "Hello?"

KIM: (*Breathless*) "Hi Mom! It's me!"

MOM: "Hi honey. How are you?"

KIM: "I'm exhausted! All I do is rush around and I still can't get everything done! I'm going crazy!"

MOM: "Oh, it's Miss Aries! Why don't you slow down a little—"

KIM: "Slow *down*? Are you kidding? I can't accomplish everything as it is!"

MOM: "I mean, why don't you plan a little less each day so you don't pressure yourself so much? You're always so pressured—"

KIM: "I'm not *pressured*! You know I *like* to have a lot of balls in the air!"

MOM: "But you just said—"

KIM: "Would you like to have dinner? How about pasta?"

MOM: "Dinner? Tonight?"

KIM: "Tonight! Right now! How soon can you be ready?"

MOM: "Well, I don't have any plans . . ."

KIM: "Great! How about Fred's? It's right around the corner. We could meet in twenty minutes. No! Make it ten!"

MOM: "Okay, but honey, drive carefully!"

KIM: "Mom, please! I'm forty years old!"

This scenario occurred regularly. Of course, I realize that my mother's advice was very sound, and I do work (when I have the time!) toward creating more tranquility and peace in my life.

The twelve astrological birth signs are as follows.

Aries	March 21–April 20
Taurus	April 21–May 21
Gemini	May 22–June 21
Cancer	June 22–July 23
Leo	July 24–August 23
Virgo	August 24–September 23
Libra	September 24–October 23
Scorpio	October 24–November 22
Sagittarius	November 23–December 21
Capricorn	December 22–January 20
Aquarius	January 21–February 19
Pisces	February 20–March 20

You might find it interesting and informative to learn more about your astrological background. To do so, consider having a chart prepared by an experienced astrologer. There are also a number of good books written by astrologists that are readily available in bookstores and libraries. Two of my favorites, *Sun Signs* and *Love Signs*, were written by author Linda Goodman.

🦅 CHOOSING YOUR RACE AND RELIGION 🦅

Throughout history, our choice of race and religion has played a crucial role in how we may be inspired to grow and mature spiritually. The earthly plane has always been a hotbed of intolerance, ignorance, and fear, as individuals of lowly enlightenment struggle to lift themselves above issues like cruel and petty prejudices, which have sometimes led to unspeakable injustices.

While still safely existing in the confines of heaven, we often optimistically decide to be reborn during periods of alarming intolerance, ensuring the advancement of our spiritual enlightenment.

Typically, if a spiritual being needs to work through issues of prejudice, intolerance, or ignorance, he may, upon his return to earth, intentionally plan to enhance his limited awareness by *knowingly* choosing a particular race or religion because of the hardship it will cause him.

Being a victim of ignorance and brutality has a profound effect on a human being's ability to build upon his existing levels of sympathy, compassion, and sensitivity toward others.

If you currently harbor prejudices against other people because of their race or religion, it's time to take those issues into consideration and begin to work on resolving them right now.

By contrast, if you find yourself a victim of prejudice because of your background, remember that you *deliberately chose* your race and/or religion to experience those issues firsthand, in order to increase your existing levels of tolerance, acceptance, and compassion toward your fellow man. We tend to learn very quickly when we are on the receiving end of such harsh and hurtful treatment, and it takes enormous courage to rise above the injustices we encounter with grace and dignity.

CHOOSING YOUR SOCIOECONOMIC BACKGROUND

Another variable we must consider is our economic background, and how privilege, or lack thereof, will help inspire us to best work through our issues and achieve our life's work.

Many spiritual beings believe that if an individual is born into poverty on the earthly plane, he will be much more inspired to make something of himself just in an effort to escape the hunger, insecurity, and want of a poverty-ridden existence. That is essentially the reason so many more people are born into destitution than into prosperity.

You may be surprised to learn that being born into significant wealth carries with it tremendous disadvantages, as it can rob an individual of his identity and initiative by overshadowing his life in a way that less-privileged individuals couldn't imagine.

For example, would you really want to trade your irreverent and happily anonymous childhood, no matter how humble, for one in which you were born into a royal monarchy to be heir to a throne? Not in your right mind, you wouldn't! Can you imagine, as a child, being thrust into the overwhelming responsibility and sacrifice of such a humorless life, and suffering the complete loss of so many freedoms that the rest of us take for granted? You see why so many spiritual beings choose to be born into poverty on the earthly plane? You have nowhere to go but up! The opportunity to prove yourself is not nearly as great if everything you want and need is in effortless abundance.

🐦 CHOOSING YOUR BIRTHPLACE 🐦

What a glorious decision! You may choose to be born anywhere on the planet. Consider the very diverse lifestyle opportunities you'd experience if you were born in Zaire, Paris, Manila, Seattle, Leningrad, Baghdad, Stockholm, Belfast, Palermo, or Buenos Aries. During this important decision-making process, you have the chance to be born wherever best suits your special requirements in terms of accomplishing your spiritual destiny.

Take a moment and recall the place where you chose to be born in this lifetime. Why do you think you chose it? Are you still living there? Is so, why? If you have moved away from your place of birth, what was the reason? Would you ever consider returning? Answers to these questions will help provide a sense of continuity as you build greater spiritual self-awareness.

CHOOSING YOUR SPIRITUAL CONTRACTS

Once you have independently established all the other dynamics of your destiny, you are finally ready to commune with other spiritual beings who are also planning their upcoming earthly vacations. It is at this time that we begin to form the commitments that evolve into learning experiences or soul-mate relationships.

We select our parents, siblings, spouse(s), close friends, business colleagues, and all others who will play a significant role in our future physical life. In addition, if we plan to be adopted, we must decide upon a biological mother and father, as well as our choice for adoptive parent(s). If we so desire, we also have the wonderful opportunity to participate in a multiple birth. With an increasing number of twins, triplets, and quadruplets being born these days because of so many more women taking fertility drugs, the chances for souls to return en masse is greater than ever before.

How do we enter into a spiritual contract with another being? How do we interact with others to make these very important decisions? Let's eavesdrop on a typical heavenly conversation between spiritual beings at the time of preparing for an earthly vacation. For clarity, I'm referring to these spiritual beings as Rachel, Michael, and William.

RACHEL: "Hi, Michael! I heard you're returning to earth."

MICHAEL: "Rachel, I was looking for you! It's true. I'm going to be born next January. I heard you're going back, too. Would you like to be my sister again?"

RACHEL: "I'd love to! But I'm not planning to make my transition back to earth for several years."

MICHAEL: "Perfect! I need to return to earth in a hurry. I've decided that my life's work will be to discover a cure for breast cancer, and I'm eager to get started."

RACHEL: "Then you can be my big brother this time. If it's okay with you, I'd like to have a sister, too. How would you feel about my approaching Jenny, who was our sister in that lifetime in Pompeii? We all had such a beautiful existence before the eruption of Mount Vesuvius—"

MICHAEL: "Fine with me, as long as I get to go first. I've already chosen Elizabeth and John for my parents. Do you remember them? They were our parents in the lifetime we shared during the French Revolution."

RACHEL: "I'd love to have them as parents again!"

MICHAEL: "Since you're going to be my sister, would you help me work through a learning disability I've chosen as a childhood issue?"

RACHEL: "Of course I will. As my brother, will you help me with my issues of independence, empowerment, and self-esteem?"

MICHAEL: "You want me to help you with those issues again? You still haven't worked them through? After all these lifetimes?"

RACHEL: "I'll have you know I've worked very hard on those issues since the last time we were together on earth. I just have some loose ends to tie up. I'll plan for Elizabeth and John to help me build good self-esteem while I'm still a little girl."

MICHAEL: "I'll be happy to help, too. Rachel, here comes William. I wonder if he's going back?"

WILLIAM: "I've been looking for both of you. I hear you're going back to earth. Mike, is it true you've chosen medicine as your life's work?"

RACHEL: "Yes, he has! And we've just decided to be brother and sister again."

WILLIAM: "That's great. I know you two have a special affinity for one another. Mike, I'm going into medicine, too. I plan to start a private practice, but I'm also going into research to study epidemic viruses. Why don't we plan to meet in medical school and eventually go into practice together?"

MICHAEL: "Sounds great! I really respected the work you did before in that lifetime as Louis Pasteur."

WILLIAM: "Then we're set! You like the idea of Harvard for medical school? We could meet there, in say, twenty-five years?"

MICHAEL: "Works for me."

WILLIAM: "Rachel, have you resolved your issues with self-esteem yet?"

RACHEL: "Not quite, but I will as a child in this next lifetime. Have you resolved your issues with commitment?"

WILLIAM: "No, but I've just finished talking with Susan, and we plan to be married again. She's agreed to be my first wife."

RACHEL: "I remember Susan. Doesn't she have commitment issues, too?"

WILLIAM: "Yes, she does. That's why we've chosen to be together again. We'll help each other. I promised to be her first husband. Our relationship will be a learning experience for both of us. Very argumentative, just like before, but it will help us mature. After I've resolved my issues with commitment, I'll finally be ready to have a heart, mind, body, and soul relationship."

RACHEL: "I'm very happy for you."

WILLIAM: "Would you consider being my second wife? If you can get through your issues of self-esteem in childhood, and I can resolve my issue of commitment with Susan, then we'll have a chance to build a soul-mate relationship. We could have a happy, long-term marriage."

RACHEL: "Considering the life's work you're planning, I'd better have my self-esteem issues resolved! Yes, William, I'd be very interested in marrying you. It would be our first opportunity to be romantic soul mates! When do you think you'll be ready for me?"

WILLIAM: "Susan and I expect to be married in our mid-twenties and remain together for about ten years. By the time my commitment issues are resolved, I'll probably be close to forty. Is that timing a problem for you?"

RACHEL: "Then I'll be close to my mid-thirties. Perfect! It will give me just enough time to get established in my life's work as an entrepreneur. Will you be interested in having children with me?"

WILLIAM: "Absolutely. Susan and I decided not to have children in this next lifetime. But I'd love to have a family with you. Why don't we plan to have three children?"

RACHEL: "It's a date! But how will we meet on the earthly plane?"

MICHAEL: "Hey, I have an idea. Will, since you and I are going to medical school and then starting a practice together, I'll be able to keep tabs on your schedule. Why don't I bring you and Rachel together? After your split with Susan, I'll introduce you to my little sister. Maybe I could arrange a blind date."

WILLIAM: "I like that idea. Then it's only a matter of time before she falls for me like a ton of bricks. Rachel, remember that lifetime when I was a military officer and you were an opera singer in Paris? I swept you off your feet. You told me you had never met anyone so handsome, so manly—''

RACHEL: ''William, you didn't tell me that you're still working through those serious issues of denial—''

MICHAEL: ''You two sound like you're already married. Could I interrupt this reminiscing long enough to remind you that we have a lot of work to do if we're going to embark on another earthly lifetime? I want to be born again, and soon! Agreed?''

RACHEL: ''Agreed!''

WILLIAM: ''Count me in!''

FINAL STAGES OF PREPARATION

After you have made all of these weighty decisions regarding the destiny of your upcoming earthly lifetime and your agenda is finalized, you are on a waiting list to return to earth. Now it is only a matter of time before your birth mother becomes pregnant. For each soul, the length of time is different; sometimes a soul will be inclined to wait patiently for years to be born to a particular mother, while in other cases, souls have the immediate advantage to return to earth to the mother of their choice.

During this waiting period, it is mandatory to participate in study groups with other heavenly beings who are also making their transition. These groups act as a primer, or preparatory class, that allows you to discuss your upcoming vacation plans, crystallizing the information inside your soul's memory bank.

Each new opportunity to return to the earthly plane is met with wild enthusiasm by a spiritual being, and by the time he begins his study group, he has already made all of the decisions he deemed necessary to allow him to be as productive as possible in terms of accruing spiritual enlightenment. He knows that his departure is imminent, and once back on the earthly plane, *he is totally on his own* in the toughest boot camp in existence. Each spiritual being decides how difficult his earthly experience will be by creating his own spiritual boot camp program, based upon what he truly believes he will be able to accomplish. The preparatory classes not only focus on further boosting each participant's level of confidence in reaching his upcoming destiny, but also serves as a sobering reminder of the adversity he may expect to encounter during his stay.

In spite of the fact that once an individual arrives on the earthly plane he is totally alone, he carries with him a powerful support system. Once on earth, an individual's soul is meant to act as a compass that will lead him in the right direction in terms of fulfilling all the dynamics of his destiny. The more an individual accesses the information held within his soul, the easier it will be to create a life on earth that is more satisfying, secure, and harmonious.

After the preparatory classes, when a spiritual being feels confident that he is ready to embark on the breath-taking journey to the earthly plane, he hovers close to his birth mother and waits for her to become pregnant. Quite often, there are other souls waiting to be born to the same mother, and returning souls often jockey for position in terms of birth order. There may be ten souls waiting, but only one, or three, or five, may actually get the opportunity. Those souls who didn't get the chance to be born to their chosen birth mother typically decide to choose again, in the hopes that another woman will present them a similar opportunity.

Surprisingly, after all of this preparation, a soul still has the opportunity to change his mind about returning to the earthly plane *even after his birth mother becomes pregnant*. This pulling back is the cause for miscarriages and stillbirths. In the event that such an episode occurs, the reticent soul will decide to either remain in heaven and depart for another life on earth at a later date, or return to the preparatory classes to more fully bolster his courage for the arduous task of returning to earth.

Although a miscarriage or stillborn child is a hideous and tragic experience for the birth mother and father, it is far better for the unprepared and frightened soul to pull back in the beginning than to move ahead with uncertainty and ruin his chances for success on the earthly plane. When a woman asks the reason behind her miscarriage or stillbirth in a private session, and she receives information about the little soul pulling back, she will most often reply, "I *felt* that! This may sound crazy, but I somehow *know* I'll be pregnant with *that child again*!" And in many cases, she is!

It is such a miraculous process when a soul returns to the earthly plane to deliberately entrust his future to you as a parent. Your child has specifically *chosen you* as a parent, and you therefore have a great responsibility to honor the spiritual contract you have with them. Many clients have asked why their children chose them as parents; some out of mere curiosity, and others out of a desire to nurture their children and facilitate their greatest spiritual growth.

But how does a parent best facilitate the spiritual growth of their child? Do you merely need to provide them with a home, proper nourishment, clothing, education, and equal parts affection and discipline? Of course, all those things are vital to your child's physical well-being. However, it is equally important for you to remember that your child chose you because he had faith and trust that you would help him achieve various parts of his spiritual destiny. Therefore, it would be very beneficial for you to discover the issues your child planned to resolve in his youth, as well as the nature of his life's work, because this awareness will allow you to best facilitate his ability to consummate his important agenda.

And now, after all the decision-making, formalizing of spiritual contracts with other returning souls, and attending classes for the earth-bound, a spiritual being is fully prepared to participate in the exciting and eventful earthly birthing process. There *is* no more luminous journey than once again making a debut on the earthly plane.

PART TWO

∽✧∾

Your Spiritual Present

FIVE

Embarking on the Journey

WHEN YOU MAKE the extraordinary journey to the earthly plane, you actually experience two moments of birth. The *physical* birth occurs when, as a tiny being, you are delivered from your mother. The moment of *spiritual* birth actually takes place at the time your soul *enters* your infant body. Each soul may decide for itself at what point it wishes to take residence in its new body, which may be at the exact moment of delivery, or up to several hours thereafter.

Just as your "deceased" loved ones and guardian angels helped in your transition 'back to the heavenly plane, they also help you to successfully venture forth for yet another challenging earthly vacation. Your soul remains fully alive and functioning while living in heaven or on earth, and during all of its transitions between the planes of existence. At no time does it lose the power of spiritual awareness.

As an infant, you can still tangibly see, hear, and touch spiritual beings. From the first moments of your arrival back to the earthly plane, you have guardian angels who are assigned to you, whose job is to provide support, protection, and encouragement as you struggle to acclimate to your new environment. Friends and family members still living in heaven work with your angels to contribute as much as possible to your initial quality of life.

One of the few guarantees a spiritual being can depend upon once back on the unpredictable earthly plane is that his soul will provide him the intuition that will help him ''see'' beyond the limits of his five senses. In fact, when you are a newborn, your soul enables you to enjoy the identical spiritual awareness you had while still a resident of the heavenly plane. Your spiritual awareness survives in its entirety, allowing a complete memory of all the issues you chose to resolve, the nature of your life's work, the purpose behind relationships with other human beings, and all the other vital dynamics of your spiritual destiny.

The experience of the soul *departing* your physical body at the time of transition is identical to your soul's *entry into* a physical body at the moment of birth. The event is swift and effortless, taking place in a mere flash of a second. But unlike the glorious release felt when your soul *departs* a physical body, your soul's *entry* into a tiny newborn body signals a drastic shift, as you immediately surrender control of your mobility, coordination, freedom, and independence.

To further complicate matters, your existing levels of wisdom, enlightenment, and maturity that have been so hard-earned in previous lifetimes become invisible except to those human beings who are unusually intuitive or spiritually perceptive. Unfortunately, unlike in heaven, you are not instantly recognized on the earthly plane for who and what you are spiritually.

As a new arrival on the earthly plane, you are regarded as a blank slate, an empty vessel devoid of any spiritual, emotional, mental, or physical capabilities, enlightenment, awareness, or understanding.

Moreover, at the same time your soul enters the physical body you have chosen, you are promptly bombarded by a series of physical sensations that are often initially frightening and disconcerting.

Imagine that you have just made your departure from heaven, where you have all the wisdom of the universe at your fingertips, where each soul is loving and supportive, where you enjoy total independence, and may spontaneously create anything you desire. Arriving on the earthly plane, you now exist as a completely helpless infant, your soul locked inescapably inside a shockingly heavy, cumbersome physical body that forces you to depend on other human beings for every necessity.

At first, the sensation of experiencing things *physically* from inside a human body is altogether unpleasant. The air feels uncomfortably chilly against your delicate skin. You cope with pangs of hunger and you're forced to consume whatever nourishment is offered whether you can tolerate it or not. The waste you have eliminated remains uncomfortably clinging to your backside inside a diaper until you are cleaned and changed.

Likewise, it is impossible to exercise any control over your physical body. If you have decided to experience an illness or health condition as an infant, you must endure these agonies with helpless suffering. Perhaps most frustrating is the fact that you cannot *communicate* what you need because it may take several years before you have a rudimentary command of the language in this hostile new environment. For years after your birth, you remain utterly dependent on those whom you chose as parents, and they are entirely responsible for every single one of your physical, emotional, mental, and spiritual daily requirements.

Even in the best of circumstances, the earthly plane

is an unpredictable destination for any soul. I often find myself looking at babies in strollers and observing their facial expressions. Have you ever noticed that some babies appear so brooding, sullen, or depressed? I always wonder if they're thinking, "What have I done? What was I thinking? I hate the earthly plane! I can't adjust to this physical body! I can't communicate! No one in this outpost of civilization understands me! Beam me back up! Get me out of here!" And whenever I see a baby who appears naturally gregarious and cheerful, I believe them to be thinking, "I'm so happy to be here on earth again! I get so much attention! I love being hugged and cuddled and kissed! This physical body is fun! The world is my oyster! I waited so long for this opportunity, and I'm going to make the most of it!"

In fact, a child's earliest quality of life hinges on, and parallels, the spiritual destiny he chose to experience during his earthly vacation. When a baby is born with physical impairments or health problems, it is the *child himself* who has chosen the condition as an issue to be experienced very early upon his arrival to the earthly plane. In truth, *many* souls plan a number of serious issues to actually begin during infancy, and this accounts for the incidence of childhood neglect, abandonment, abuse, and illness. Confronting issues so early on allows an individual to accomplish as much as possible during his brief earthly visit and return to his home in heaven a much stronger, compassionate, resilient, and enlightened being.

The souls who choose to encounter such sobering issues while still in childhood must carefully select parents who will present them with the circumstances necessary to facilitate their intended spiritual growth and development. For example, an individual deciding to endure a birth defect or serious childhood illness will often choose parents who are giving, selfless, compassionate, loving, and supportive, to best guide them through the terrible ordeal.

By contrast, in some earthly lifetimes, when a soul is planning to encounter and resolve traumatic issues, he will search for prospective parents who are themselves extremely dysfunctional, and who will create a home environment teeming with issues such as control, abandonment, neglect, addiction, or abuse.

Consider your own childhood for a moment. Remember that you intentionally chose your parents because of what they could contribute to your spiritual development. This new awareness may help to change your attitude and perception about what you've experienced as a child, especially if you had to deal with significant dysfunction. Remember that you *expected* to face the adversity you encountered because it was necessary for you to gain the strength and maturity that has allowed you to become the person you are today. If you came from a dysfunctional home, you had the spiritual *advantage* of starting to address your issues while very young, rather than waiting until adulthood when adversity seems so much more difficult to accept or resolve.

How could issues appear *more* traumatic in adulthood, when you have the maturity and freedom to deal with them as you see fit? Children acclimate much faster to transition than do adults, and are far more forgiving, tolerant, and nonjudgmental. Therefore, they are more likely to release the haunting memories of bitterness, betrayal, anger, or lack of trust that is so often a result of living with dysfunction. By acknowledging and resolving issues in early childhood, you have the distinct advantage of healing faster emotionally and spiritually than you might as an adult. Considering the fact that issues are always, without exception, worked through by encountering adversity, and the adversity must be resolved in the small window of time you've allotted for this lifetime, wouldn't you prefer to address your serious issues right away to get them out of the way? Isn't it always easier to handle dreaded tasks as soon as possible to eliminate the anxiety they cause?

Therefore, if you had a childhood filled with dysfunction, you might want to consider the fact that it was a precious opportunity to expand your existing levels of spiritual enlightenment. As an adult, if you find yourself continually haunted by painful childhood memories, you may want to consider therapy to help you finally release the old emotional baggage that could be sabotaging your personal and professional success. In many instances, we can heal childhood wounds on our own, but if you have already reached adulthood and have not yet completed your healing, chances are you'll need outside support. By understanding what you've experienced as a child and the reasons behind why you *chose* that for yourself, you'll be cleansing your heart and soul of past hurts that will finally allow you to live totally in the present without your childhood experiences limiting current and future relationships.

One of the most baffling circumstances encountered by a young soul on the earthly plane is that he is expected to conform to the spiritual, emotional, mental, and physical sensibilities, behaviors, and beliefs held by the rest of his new family and/or community.

In heaven, each spiritual being is celebrated for his unique gifts and levels of enlightenment. Conversely, once reborn on the earthly plane, a child quickly discovers that his spiritual individuality is looked upon with outright suspicion by the adults and older children of the household.

For example, when a child discusses his imaginary playmates, who are, incidentally, spiritual beings, an adult is likely to respond, ''Okay, honey, that's nice. Now finish your vegetables!'' or ''Honey, you know

there *isn't any such thing!* If you had more friends your
own age, you wouldn't need to create *imaginary* playmates!''

At the same time, if a child discloses a recent conversation with a deceased relative or family friend, an
adult or older sibling is likely to respond, ''What? *Aunt
Grace* talked to you last night in your room? But that's
impossible! You know she's *dead!* She can't talk to *anyone* any more!'' or ''*Grandpa* came to see you when
you were *playing outside*? I know you miss him, but
he's in *heaven*. He can't come back ever again!''

Furthermore, when a child reveals the information that
is naturally flowing from his soul, he is the recipient of
even more negativity, because an adult or older sibling
is likely to respond, ''*You're* going to be an *astronaut*
when you grow up? Ha! That's a joke!'' or ''You *remember* fighting in World War I as an ace flyer? I'm
going to talk to your mother about getting you some
therapy!'' or ''*You* think you're going to be *winning an
Olympic medal* when you're eighteen? You can't even
walk across a room without tripping! Now go make your
bed!'' or ''You think that someday you're going to
marry Douglas from next door? That's so cute! Listen
everybody, my little girl has her first crush!''

This negativity is confusing to a small child, as it directly contradicts all of the existing spiritual awareness
inside his soul that is guiding him toward his intended
destiny. The adult opposition also threatens communication between the child and his guardian angels and
other spiritual beings. Once a child experiences this negativity, he will often alter his behavior to conform to the
demands of his family members. When a child forces
himself to conform, he begins to lose pieces of his identity. In doing so, he begins to erase the memory of his
spiritual destiny, a process I call spiritual amnesia.

Spiritual amnesia results from an early home envi-

*ronment in which a child is not encouraged or supported
to communicate the awareness from his soul, or share
the information he receives from his angels or other
spiritual beings.*

It takes years to develop spiritual amnesia, and little
by little, this process results in a complete memory loss
of an individual's chosen destiny, including life's work,
issues to be resolved, and spiritual contracts. As self-
destructive as it may be, it is very common for a child
to gradually detach from the heavenly plane in an attempt to emotionally survive while on an earthly vacation. When this occurs, he is very much like a ship
without a compass, floundering in an open sea with no
purpose or direction. When an individual shuts down the
information from his soul and his ability to receive intuitive guidance, the spiritual journey becomes more difficult. I would compare this situation to embarking on a
road trip without any idea of how to drive, where you
are headed, who should be going with you, or how long
you will be gone.

Many of my clients who are parents have shared sto-
ries with me about their child's astonishing intuitive abilities, and how, often on a daily basis, the child describes
his awareness about his future path, a dream in which
he has received clairvoyant information, or his encounters with spiritual beings. It's very commonplace for a
deceased family member to begin a relationship with a
child in order to love, guide, support, nurture, or simply
play with him.

Children who have never had the opportunity to interact or even hear about Grandpa Ed, or Aunt Sally,
will earnestly disclose that the deceased family member
came for a visit and talked with them. Although the deceased family member passed back to heaven before
they were even born, the children are able to fully describe the individual's appearance and reveal entire con-
versations about topics that they couldn't have possibly

known about otherwise. Typically, the deceased family member will ask the child to pass along a series of messages to adults who are too closed or blocked to receive it for themselves.

What can you do to support a child's natural intuitive abilities that can allow him to trust in what he receives from his inner self, or his soul, as well as maintain his respect for the spiritual beings who regularly communicate with him? Develop an ongoing rapport with your child from the time he is very young, and encourage him to discuss the spiritual truths, or encounters, he experiences both during waking hours and in his dreams. If he knows you are open and eager to hear about what he is sensing, he won't feel the need to ignore or dismiss the valuable information from his soul or from his angels, and he'll never feel compelled to begin the process of spiritual amnesia. Your child's self-awareness will remain intact, allowing him to acknowledge his special individuality, which will nurture his self-esteem and confidence. In addition, he'll be more likely to live his life as a *feeler* rather than a *thinker*, which will help him enjoy emotional intimacy and commitment with others as an adult. He will also have an unwavering focus on his life's work and the issues he is to resolve, which will save him years of searching for the answers to who he is and what he is supposed to be doing with his life.

If you feel that you have developed spiritual amnesia because you aren't completely certain about who you are, why you are here, or where the dickens you are going, take heart! Although you may have been living with a terminal case of spiritual amnesia for years, rest assured that it's very easy to recover your soul memory and learn to communicate with your angels and other spiritual beings.

Now you have a better understanding about why this earthly plane is such a difficult one to get accustomed to! It is such an arduous task to keep putting one foot in front of the other to accomplish the goals on our spiritual agenda, that I believe we're all entitled to feel very sorry for ourselves from time to time. Spend a moment and pat yourself on the back in tribute to everything you *have* already achieved.

Now let's discuss exactly *how* you can erase your spiritual amnesia and learn to access all the personal information that is stored within your soul.

SIX

❦

Using Your Soul as a Compass

DO YOU REALIZE how divine you are? Are you aware that you possess an inner radiance that transcends your outer appearance and mental aptitude? You are a truly luminous being, whose incandescence is powerful enough to cast a beacon of light over the shadows of the earthly plane. You have the power to provide a spiritual sustenance to those living in fear and ignorance, the ability to ignite a spiritual passion in others that reflects your own enlightenment, and the courage that can inspire others to stand beside you and realize the scope of their own inner strength and beauty.

You have something inside you that is more beautiful than you could ever imagine, something that glows with the infinite wisdom achieved throughout all of its spiritual journeys. This inner piece of you is given to you directly by God, intended to eternally mirror his presence, and reflect what you have accomplished in your thousands of earthly lifetimes.

God's endowment serves as your compass, as well as

your diary. It directs and guides your journeys on the earthly plane, while recording every experience and encounter that adds to your burgeoning levels of maturity, wisdom, and enlightenment. This endowment is your strongest, most enduring lifeline to the heavenly plane and is the very essence of your being. It is your soul.

While you live in heaven, you exist at the highest level of your being, unencumbered by troublesome issues, and free from the responsibility of maintaining a physical body. Your soul joyfully interacts with others who are also living at the highest level of their enlightenment.

During a vacation to earth's spiritual boot camp, your soul is the primary tether to the heavenly plane. It serves as your internal compass because it has an infinite memory of your unique spiritual identity. Your spiritual identity is comprised of specific information that includes *where* you came from, *who* you are, *why* you are here in this lifetime, *what* you are supposed to be accomplishing in terms of spiritual agenda, and *when* you should be reaching your goals. As you venture forth to achieve your spiritual agenda, your soul busily records all the details of every single experience and encounter in each lifetime spent on the earthly plane.

In childhood, each of us maintains a complete awareness of our spiritual identity because the soul is consistently flooding us with information about who we are and why we are here. For whatever reason, if an individual begins to deny or dismiss the information coming from his soul, it eventually slows to a trickle, and then shuts down entirely.

How do you know if you have unknowingly shut down the information from your soul? Consider the following questions.

- Are you aware of receiving ''gut'' instincts?
- If so, do you listen to them?
- If you are aware of inner intuitive feelings, do you trust them enough to follow through with what they tell you?
- Are you more mental than emotional?
- Do you dismiss other people's intuitive feelings?
- Are you aware of your life's work?
- Are you conscious of the issues you have to resolve?
- Do you understand the purpose behind your important relationships?
- Do you understand why you have encountered the stumbling blocks that represent patterns of difficulty in your life?
- Do you take time to consider the messages conveyed in your nightly dreams?
- Do you have any clue as to the nature of your past lifetimes?
- Do you consistently feel energized, happy, and moving forward with purpose and direction?
- Do you currently feel you have positive things to look forward to that make your life truly worth living?

If you have answered ''no'' to more than *one* of these questions, you can safely assume that you've slowed, or entirely shut down the information coming from your soul.

Other symptoms of spiritual amnesia include fatigue, depression, sleeplessness, feeling as though you're simply going through the motions, hopelessness about your future, an inability to relate to others with genuine emotional intimacy, confusion about why you are here in this lifetime and why you're surrounded by such difficult people, as well as the desire to end this earthly lifetime.

If you can admit that you are able to relate to some or all of these symptoms, you're actually taking a very positive step in improving your quality of life. The first step of any spiritual journey is becoming aware of where you are and where you would like to be. If you recognize spiritual amnesia as a current problem for you, this is a wonderful new awareness. You now have a starting point for your journey. The destination that I want to help you reach is the ability to again experience a clear stream of self-awareness coming directly from your soul's memory bank. You'll be able to access information about where you've been, who you are, why you are here, and where you are going.

To begin the process of encouraging your soul to re-open its memory, you must start with some troubleshooting that will save you from unintentionally sabotaging your first few steps.

There are two bases of operation within every human being. The mental base of operation is our tendency to use logic, empirical reasoning, and cautious reserve when making decisions and relating to others. The emotional base of operation is our tendency to demonstrate emotional openness and expressiveness, spontaneity, and intuitiveness when making decisions and relating to others.

Individuals who embrace a more emotional approach to life have a *much* easier time accessing soul memory, because the soul floods information through the heart in the way of *feelings*. Therefore, if you routinely listen to and trust in your feelings, you are already in touch with your soul. If, however, you dismiss your feelings and instead focus mainly on logic, you'll need to practice to open up to your feelings, which will allow you to access your soul's memory bank.

How do you know if you're more of a mental person

than an emotional person? Chances are, you've become very familiar with the base of operation that suits you best. Men, by the way, have more of a tendency to gravitate toward the "mental." If you are a man, just ask the women in your life. Wives, sisters, daughters, mothers, and even your close female business associates would probably be most happy to give you their opinion, as women tend to be very eager to emotionally mentor the men in their lives. Just make certain you're prepared to get an honest opinion from them! Most likely, if you feel the need to *ask*, you're already aware that you *are* a little on the mental side, and could benefit from opening up emotionally.

What can you do to open up emotionally? First, you may want to consider that being emotionally expressive and responsive is a *lifestyle* that will take some commitment on your part to achieve. But understand that moving your current base of operation from your head to your heart is not an impossible goal, and with a little effort, can be quickly achieved.

For instance, as a mental person, you are more disposed to rely on your logic. In doing so, you are unknowingly expending enormous levels of energy attempting to dismiss or ignore what your feelings are trying to tell you. Try to reverse the process. Focus on what your *feelings* are conveying, and strive to dismiss and ignore your mental thought processes. Does that idea frighten you? Expect it to, because you've been relying on your logic as a haven safe from emotional confusion, hurts, or rejection. Let me explain why you may want to strongly consider leaving this predictable, safe haven for an existence in which you're flooded by a constant stream of ever-changing and unpredictable emotional and intuitive feelings.

First, you'll begin to enjoy a much closer relationship with those people in your life, particularly women and children, who are themselves emotional. You'll learn to comfortably give and receive emotional affection, and this will have a profound impact on the quality of your relationships. In addition, you'll discover how creative and intuitive you really are, and learn to exploit these newfound talents and abilities to grow dramatically.

Risk-taking and decision-making will suddenly appear so much easier because as a feeler, you'll be able to take far greater risks with all of the encouragement coming from your heart. By listening to and trusting in this information, you'll assuredly earn far greater personal and professional rewards. You'll also embrace a far greater level of spontaneity, which will expand your horizons to lead you to explore new activities and enterprises that will make your life more stimulating.

Your sex life will improve as well, because you'll be sharing another dimension of yourself with your partner, inspiring them to greater heights of abandon. And if all these benefits weren't convincing enough, perhaps the most important reason to become more emotional is that you'll easily be able to access information from your soul.

Let's assume that you've worked to develop an emotional base of operation, and are now ready to access information coming directly from your soul. Don't be concerned that because you haven't been listening to your soul it can't be jump-started. As soon as you start requesting information, it will begin to provide you with a slow trickle of awareness. If you continue to ask for and utilize the information you receive, your soul will steadily increase its communication until you are once again flooded with awareness.

But how can you determine whether you are receiving information from your heart or your head? When you're faced with a decision, it is very common to find yourself caught between your heart, with all of its feelings, and your head, with all of its thoughts. This internal argument may become utterly confusing and derailing, preventing you from making any decision at all. The following is an example of such an argument.

HEART/SOUL: "I'm miserable and bored with my job at ABC Company. I just *know* I should start my own business."

HEAD: "Are you *crazy*? *Leave a secure job*? We should *retire* from this company! We'll have a good pension."

HEART/SOUL: "*Retire* from ABC? I can't stand working there *another month*! I've *always* wanted my own business. I can use my nest egg to open it—and my best friend Carol would make a great business partner. She's excited about it, too, and has already secured commitments from several large companies who have agreed to be our initial clients!"

HEAD: "Use the *nest egg*? We'll be broke and living in the gutter! We'll be homeless with no retirement money! What if Carol doesn't come through? What if the clients decide not to pay their bills? What about paying rent? And keeping up with all the other monthly bills? There's no *guarantee* it'll be successful! We *can't* do something that *isn't guaranteed*!"

HEART/SOUL: "Oh-oh! What if I *do* lose all of my savings? I worked *so hard* for that money. But if I don't take the risk *now*, then *when*? I feel so strongly that if I stay with ABC for another year, I'll be stuck there *forever*!"

HEAD: "Good! It's *dependable security*!"

HEART/SOUL: "But I'm not earning very much! There's not much hope for a promotion or a salary increase. Hey, this conversation is familiar! We've had this argument *before*! Last year! And the year before that! And the year before *that*! You keep telling me not to follow my dreams.''

HEAD: ''So *what*? ABC is *dependable*! We shouldn't take the risk. *Any* risk-taking is *unnecessary*. Remember the risk you took five years ago by getting married? How did that turn out?''

HEART/SOUL: ''Well, even though it turned out to be a learning experience, I truly felt it was right at the time.''

HEAD: ''And now you *feel* this is right! You and your *feelings*! You could be wrong again!''

HEART/SOUL: ''Oh my gosh, my head is probably right. What if I *am* wrong? I felt so *positive* about it, but maybe I just don't have what it takes to start my own business! I've always *hated* my job, but I guess I could stay at ABC for a little while longer until I figure out what to do. I'll have to call Carol and tell her to go ahead without me. Now I'm so *depressed*! And I feel so *tired*! Where did I put those damn *Oreos*?''

I'm sure that you can relate to this argument and have actually participated in such a defeating dialogue. Your logical side will always steer you away from taking any risks whatsoever, but your life's journey is made up of nothing *but* new challenges that take the form of risks. Do you understand how trusting and relying solely on your head can result in needless turmoil, friction, and fear? If you develop a system that will allow you to tune out these derailing thoughts, then these internal arguments will completely come to an end.

One of the simplest, most effective methods for accomplishing this is to pretend that your brain is an entity outside yourself. To turn off all of the negative mental chatter, simply say, ''Brain, shut off.'' It's that easy. I usually have to tell my brain to be quiet several times before it will obediently shut down. And *don't wait* until your heart and your head get into an argument! Once your mind talks you into a very worrisome state, it will be that much *more* difficult to stop the process. I recommend that you get in the routine of turning off your negative thoughts the *moment* they begin. In fact, some of my more ''mental'' clients have developed the wonderful habit of telling their brain to shut off the second they wake up in the morning and the last thing before they go to sleep at night.

You may now be wondering how to differentiate the information that comes from your heart/soul, from the information that comes from your head. The information that comes from your heart/soul will always be positive, optimistic, self-loving, and will encourage you to *move forward*. The information that comes from your head will be self-critical, negative, pessimistic, and will frighten you into believing you shouldn't make any decision, take any risk, or engage in any forward movement, *ever.* My clients regularly ask if it is possible to be a purely mental person and develop a spectacular quality of life. The answer is quite simple. You can't! The only way to develop a fulfilling life is to regularly engage in the sort of soul-propelled risk-taking that will allow you to *move away* from your current existence to cross over new and different thresholds.

Don't be concerned that if you tell your brain to shut off, you won't have your full mental capacities available to you any time you wish. Keep in mind that your brain is not the center for creativity, intuitiveness, emotional expressiveness, or sexual abandon. All those fabulous traits and abilities come from the heart and soul. Besides causing the mental chatter that keeps you from changing your life for the better, your brain really serves very few purposes beyond balancing a checkbook. Make the attempt to keep your brain turned off for one week. If you're like most people, you'll be shocked at how your self-critical, defeatist, negative, and pessimistic thought processes simply melt away, leaving you happier, more at peace, more confident, and full of physical energy. You have nothing to lose, and everything to gain!

Now that we've discussed how mental chatter disables your ability to receive information from your soul, and you've learned how to turn down the negative thought processes, we're ready to explore soul communication.

How will you recognize when your soul is communicating with you? It's very simple. You will feel flooded with emotions that represent everything from past life experiences, relationships with others, your life's work, issues still to be resolved, and information about your health and well-being.

Almost without exception, all of the emotions that bubble up from inside of you come from the soul. Therefore, you're always on the right track spiritually if you pay attention to what your *feelings* are telling you. The more open you are to your feelings, the greater the flood of intuitiveness from your soul. Generally, people who have always been "feelers" have mastered their ability to make decisions and take risks because from experience, they firmly *believe* in the positive information they receive from within. Some people call their soul information "gut instincts," or intuitiveness, while others describe it as "second sight."

Your heart and soul will always recommend, support, and encourage positive action to help you move your life into more satisfying directions. Your head will consistently reinforce a type of negative, self-defeating mindset that will frighten you into hesitating, until ultimately, you choose to do nothing at all.

Whenever I have a private channeling session with an individual who is more of a feeler than a thinker, and he asks about the nature of his life's work, he is rarely surprised by the information that is revealed. He will often exclaim, "That's my dream! That's exactly what I've always wanted to do with my life!" In other words, if you are a feeler, it is very likely you have already become familiar with the information from your soul's memory bank and accept it as your truth.

For instance, what does your soul tell you about the nature of your life's work? What are your dreams or fantasies about the "perfect" career for you? If your dreams are springing from inside your heart/soul, then you can rest assured that they represent your spiritual destiny and you may trust them implicitly. You simply wouldn't feel as *passionate* about something that wasn't right for you.

Accordingly, you may also receive information from your soul about the nature of your past earthly lifetimes. Your soul provides your sense of déjà vu, and reminds you about talents and abilities you've mastered in previous incarnations. For instance, do you have a passion for the island of Capri? Dancing the tango? Snow skiing? Eating Thai food? Listening to classical music? Investing in the stock market? Writing? If you have a *passion* for places, people, things, or activities, chances are that you've loved them before in a past lifetime. The memory of all you've done before is securely stored inside your soul's memory bank.

The energy from your soul flows outward to encircle your physical body, filling what you would refer to as your private space. Although at times, we may receive incredibly strong intuitive impulses about people or places that we see on television, or at a distance, we have a far greater intuitive experience when we interact with other people up close.

When you are privy to someone's soul energy, you can learn quite a bit about them intuitively. For example, you'll be able to discover if you've had a positive past-life experience with them if you feel emotionally warm when you interact with their soul's energy. You'll know that you had a negative past-life experience with them if you feel distrustful, nervous, or negative when approaching them. If you feel absolutely nothing when standing in their soul energy, you might assume that you've never met them in a past incarnation.

In those first moments when romantic soul mates are reunited on the earthly plane, it is commonplace for one or both parties to immediately recognize the other and say to themselves, "I'm going to marry this person!" An individual would be privy to that sudden awareness because he would be flooded with information from his own soul.

There is a reason that your soul's energy extends out from your body. It *attracts* those individuals who are meant to have a purpose in your life, while it *discourages* those who have no spiritual contract with you.

At this juncture, we are ready to begin exploring my techniques for helping restore and maintain a natural flood of intuitiveness from your soul's memory bank.

To begin, you'll need to move to a quiet environment, away from radio, television, and any interruption. It would also be a good idea to turn off your telephone. The moment you begin these exercises, inevitably your phone will start jangling and you won't be able to get anything accomplished. I also recommend that you sit in a comfortable chair, or on a couch, because if you lie down, it's very possible you'll drift off to sleep! In addition, make certain that you're not hungry, physically exhausted, or emotionally upset, because those distractions will also derail your progress. You might feel a little nervous about attempting this exercise the first few times, but rest assured that you'll develop more confidence as you rebuild a relationship with your soul. Nervousness will not prevent you from being successful with these exercises.

The goal of this exercise is to jump-start information from your soul's memory bank. Every time you practice the technique, plan to ask three questions of your soul that represent your biggest priorities. You may ask about your life's work, past lifetimes, the purpose of certain relationships, or any other piece of information that is relevant to building your spiritual self-awareness. Consider what questions are most interesting to you *before* you begin. Once you have decided on your questions, you're ready to get acquainted with your soul!

Gently shut your eyes and keep them closed during the entire exercise. Take the time necessary to develop a small sense of peacefulness. Let the peacefulness wash over you and envelop you with a calming security. Tell yourself that you are safe, secure, and that nothing will harm or threaten you in any way.

In your mind, picture a flight of stairs just in front of you. At the top of the stairs is a bright blue door that is now closed. You're going to take that first step, but refrain from going any farther. You feel peace and calm. The blue door beckons you to move closer. You now move to the second step. Although you are still awash with an inner calm, you are starting to feel slight tingles of energy. It is time to move to the third step. The blue door remains closed, but now you are curious to know what lies just beyond its threshold. You move to the fourth step. The tingles of energy are now stronger. It is time to move to the fifth step. You are now halfway up the staircase. You begin to feel that there is something wonderful for you just beyond the blue door. You move to the sixth, and then the seventh steps. You feel an intense level of energy now, and the desire to cross over the blue door's threshold is almost overwhelming. You quickly scale the eighth, ninth, and tenth steps with confidence and purpose. You are now standing directly in front of the blue door. It is still closed. You're eager to explore what is behind the door. You *ask* for the big blue door to open. At your request, it opens slowly to reveal a beautiful scene. As you take that final step and cross over the door's threshold, you find yourself in a place more wonderful than you could ever have imagined, where all the answers to your questions will be available to you. You have now journeyed inside your own soul.

Take a moment and enjoy the surroundings. You may decide exactly how your environment appears. This time, you may find yourself at the seashore. Next time, in the middle of a peaceful forest. And yet another time, you may choose to visit a Tibetan monastery Or the Champs Élysée in Paris. It is your exercise and you are always free to decide which environment is most appealing each time you make the journey.

Now that you feel comfortable and are enjoying your surroundings, you may ask your first question. Ask it slowly and clearly. The answer to your question will come in mere seconds. It will come to you in the form of understanding. Tell your soul that you wish to remember what it has revealed to you.

Proceed to your second question. Again, you will have your answer in mere seconds. Ask your soul to allow you to remember what it has revealed. Then ask your third question, again requesting that you have total recall. If you have asked your questions, and you have any confusion, or wish more detailed information, simply make another request of your soul. Following your request, if the same information is repeated, or no more information is forthcoming, it means that this journey is finished. Your soul is communicating that it will not reveal any additional awareness to you at that time.

However, if you are just attempting this exercise,

don't get frustrated if the depth of information is less than you anticipated. Remember, by this time you've probably been ignoring your soul's information for years. Give yourself a reasonable amount of time to get it flowing again. The amount of time it will require will be different for each individual. The more you practice this exercise, the faster you'll be receiving very specific information that will be free-flowing all during your waking and sleeping hours. Remember that the primary objective of this process is to jump-start the soul and encourage it to flood you with information *outside* of performing this exercise.

When you have received all the soul information available to you at that time, no matter how limited you believe the level of awareness to be, be grateful to your soul for what it has revealed. Have confidence that the more you practice, the more detailed the information you'll be able to access. Before you leave your beautiful place, formally thank your soul for opening up to you. Now it is time to end the journey.

Tell yourself that you are leaving the secure confines of the environment you've imagined. Turn around, re-trace your steps until you cross back over the threshold of the blue door, and move down the ten stairs in peace and confidence. With each step, count backward from the number ten. You'll ''awaken'' once you've left the last step, feeling refreshed and peaceful, and retaining the high level of physical energy that you experienced on the journey. You will also have total and complete recall of what your soul revealed to you.

With a little practice, each time you perform this exercise, you'll awaken to discover a new level of self-awareness that will help you begin changing your life for the better!

SEVEN

❧❧❧

Living With Purpose
and Direction

YOU'VE ALREADY MADE quite a journey toward greater
spiritual awareness and enlightenment. In earlier chapters, you've learned that you came from the heavenly
plane and are here on earth in this lifetime to achieve a
specific destiny. You've also learned that you can develop a remembrance of your destiny by practicing my
simple "climbing the stairs" technique, which will allow you to erase confusion about where you are supposed to be headed, and ignore limitations you've set in
regard to your potential. Next, we're going to discuss
how you can build upon this foundation to create an
unwavering sense of momentum in your life that will be
fueled by a steadfast commitment to your individual purpose and direction.

Think of achieving your destiny, or spiritual goals, as
your *birthright* on the earthly plane. It is impossible to
fail in your quest to accomplish your spiritual goals because the path you chose is open and accessible to you,
or you wouldn't have decided to return to the earthly

plane at this time. You must have true faith that if you follow the path that represents your destiny, it will be impossible to fail. To build the greatest level of success, you need to live your life with a clear, positive focus on your spiritual goals and a resolute determination to accomplish them. By doing so, you'll create a new sense of confidence that will help fuel all of your endeavors.

Failing to acknowledge your spiritual goals is very much like getting into your car and driving with no particular destination in mind. You'll be very busy driving, but you'll never *get anywhere*. Is that how you are living your life? If so, this is a perfect time to reevaluate where your life is headed. Why is *this* a perfect time? Stating the obvious, there is no time like the present! The sooner you begin, the faster you'll feel increasing levels of success and fulfillment.

There are two vital reasons why you should become an active participant in consistent goal-setting. First, it will force you to become organized and to establish suitable priorities. Second, you'll discover how to set realistic time frames in which to achieve your goals.

The process of goal-setting will force you to focus on what you want for your future. If you've had a hard time setting goals in the past, you'll likely discover that the reason for the difficulty lies in the fact that you've been primarily concentrating on what you *don't want*. Have you ever found yourself saying, "Well, I don't know exactly where I'm going or what I *want* to do, but I can sure tell you what I *don't* want to do!"

An explicit awareness of what you *don't want* is born out of your experience with people, places, or things that have provided necessary learning experiences. Your unmistakable sense of what you don't want has its roots in past personal or professional burnout.

Although it is very important to fully understand and appreciate the lessons of the past, a prolonged fixation on them will *prevent* forward movement because instead of looking into the future, you maintain a backward focus on the past. If you find it difficult to determine what you intend to do with your life, you are most likely stuck in a learning-experience time warp, and you need to bring yourself up to the present so you may begin to concentrate on your future.

If you find that you can't set goals because you focus too much on the past, there is a big, bright light at the end of the tunnel! Don't lose sight of the fact that you have already developed the exceptional ability to *focus*, and when you feel that you really want to change your life, all you have to do is *redirect* your focus. Simply adjust your focus to the *present*, and instead of focusing on what you *don't want* any longer, ask yourself what you *do want*.

When you begin this process, your focus will naturally start to return to the past. When that happens, tell yourself that you're no longer interested in what has already occurred, and muster up the courage to remain focused on the present and the future. Initially, this may be uncomfortable, because as you become aware of how empty your current existence may be, you may fall into the self-destructive trap of complacency, thinking that, "Well, I'm lonely and unhappy, but at least my life is so much better than when I was married to so and so," or "Well, I hate my current job, but I remember how much worse my old job was and how badly my boss treated me . . ." When your thoughts of the past allow you to justify an unsatisfying present, you're sure to remain stuck exactly where you are.

Remember that you are the architect of your destiny on the earthly plane. You have the responsibility to shape your life into exactly what you most desire it to be. Your life was never meant to be a series of disasters, in which you have no power but to simply *react*. Your learning experiences were never intended to *derail* your forward movement, they were destined to *inspire* it!

You have the opportunity to *act* rather than *react,* and develop control over your life. In response, you may be thinking, "Okay, I'd love to take control over my quality of life, but *how* do I figure out what I *do want*?"

Bear in mind that you decided all of the particulars of your current destiny before you were born in this lifetime. Accordingly, you'll feel as if you are taking control of your life *only* if and when you can develop a *remembrance* of what you previously planned as your spiritual agenda. Don't make life more difficult than it really is! No matter how clueless you are about where you should be headed, don't waste your precious time and energy reinventing the wheel.

I look at life as a page in a beautiful spiritual coloring book. Thankfully, the outlines are all there. We just have to add the colors we desire to bring the page to life. The colors are symbolic of the *actions* that move our lives forward in appropriate and satisfying directions. As we *act*, we add color to the outline, and life to the page of our coloring book. But first, we must be able to recognize our outline by recalling what we originally planned for this lifetime.

Besides developing the self-awareness necessary to decipher what you *do want* and *don't want*, you should develop an understanding of the second part of the process. Once you comprehend the specifics of your destiny, and your outline takes form and structure, it is time to then call in the "big guns," or your angels, to help support your efforts. By having a discussion with them and explaining what you want and need, you'll be tapping into the most powerful source of energy in the universe, which will augment your efforts and help move things forward *much faster*.

To communicate with your angels about your goals,

simply make a written list of the specific dynamics you wish to achieve and refer to it daily. This process is called manifesting.

Manifesting refers to the practice of sending intentions out into the universe for divine guidance and assistance. Your angels have been assigned to you to help you accomplish your destiny in as timely a way as possible. Therefore, your angels remain steadfast and eager to assist your forward movement. For each step you take, they will get behind you and add to your momentum by carrying you another five steps. How do your angels carry you and help provide momentum?

Although your angels consistently maintain a presence right at your side, they wait until you develop an awareness of your destiny and then ask for specific help in achieving it. You are asking for their assistance by writing a list of what you want through the process of manifesting. By doing so, you are giving your angels the message that you're aware of where you are headed on your journey, and eager to start putting one foot in front of the other until you reach your spiritual goals. That is their cue to jump into the process and help facilitate all the dynamics of your manifesting list.

Many of my clients have asked, "But if my angels are so aware, they should already *know* what I need! Why do I have to *figure it out* and then *write it down* for them?"

Like a human friend who has developed a heightened level of spirituality, your angels will always wait to be *invited* by you to take part in the process. Remember, *this is your life.* We human beings tend to get very frustrated and feel annoyingly pressured when we're on the receiving end of help we haven't asked for. Your angels stand by and wait for you to become aware of who you are and where you are supposed to be going, so you have the desire to accomplish your spiritual agenda. The desire has to come from inside of you.

For example, have you ever had someone, no matter how good their intentions, suggest you lose weight? Or get another job? Or get a divorce? Or handle your money differently? You could love and respect the person who has given you the advice, but if it hasn't come from inside of you, there is *no way* you're going to follow through. Nor should you! And most likely, you'd be very frustrated with the person for butting in. Your angels work on the same premise.

Once you become aware of your destiny, it's time to manifest! This is an incredible exercise that you'll find fascinating and insightful. You'll have the opportunity to focus on the present and future, and really brainstorm about what you want in your life. Manifesting involves broadcasting intent into the universe for spiritual beings to begin to help you achieve your goals and aspirations. And let me say quite emphatically, that when you engage spiritual beings by asking them for help with your established destiny, things start to move forward at breakneck speed!

When I talk about *sending intent out into the universe,* I'm referring to the two-part process of developing an awareness of your destiny and then following through by *writing* your intent to achieve it.

Before you begin honing your skills, there are several important details that you must keep in mind. First, keep in mind that you'll only achieve results if you're attempting to manifest something that is currently on your spiritual agenda. In contrast, if you're trying to manifest something that is not any part of your destiny, you could manifest until you turn blue in the face and end up achieving nothing.

Let's speculate that you are determined to hold a man-

agement position for a Fortune 500 company. But because the life's work you planned for this lifetime
involves owning your own business, no matter how
much you try to manifest, you'll never get that corner
office working for someone else.

*Manifesting rule number one: If you try to manifest
something outside of what you planned for your destiny,
spiritual beings will wait to help once you are more on
track with your awareness.*

We'll also speculate that you really want a particular
relationship to work out and you decide to enlist the help
of the universe through manifesting. But this relationship
was never meant to be anything more than what you
have already experienced. No matter how much you attempt to manifest, it will have no bearing on the relationship.

Perhaps you are putting all kinds of energy out into
the universe to win the lottery or some other kind of
financial windfall. If a windfall is not on your agenda
for this lifetime, you're completely wasting your time
and effort.

*Manifesting rule number two: If you try to manifest
part of your destiny prematurely, spiritual beings will
wait to help you once you are more on track with your
awareness.*

Timing also plays a vital role in the success of your
manifesting. You may have come into an awareness of
your spiritual agenda, and invested time and energy in
manifesting these spiritual goals. But in spite of all your
efforts, what if nothing is happening and you remain
stuck where you are? *Your timing is off!*

For instance, we'll assume that you have a specific
understanding of your life's work. You practiced the
stair-climbing exercise and discovered you're supposed
to work as a writer and speaker. You *know* writing and
speaking is what you are to accomplish in this lifetime

and you're willing to do anything it takes to make it a reality. Let's even speculate that you've devoted the time and energy necessary to write a book, but you're getting nothing but rejections from literary agents and publishers. How can this rejection occur, if you are following your true path?

If you become aware of your life's work or any other dynamic on your spiritual to-do list, and are actively pursuing these goals as well as manifesting your intent, but nothing is transpiring, the timing is off. You're on the right track, but unknowingly trying to force the process. Remember that your destiny revolves around what you are to do and when you are to do it.

As with most of my lessons, I had to learn about this the hard way. When I discovered that my life's work involved writing, I was thrilled. As all writers are advised to do, I decided to write about something I knew. I had an idea for a novel, and I began to write a mystery-thriller about a psychic channel who helps the police catch a serial killer. I have worked with the police and private investigators on a variety of violent crimes including murder, sexual assault, kidnapping, and arson, as well as on missing person cases, and I believed my background would provide an authenticity that readers might find compelling. I worked for more than three years on the book and when it was finally finished, I attempted to get it published. But absolutely no one was interested in the manuscript at that time.

You may be wondering how a psychic could run into such adversity, especially having the ability to fluently channel. Throughout the three-year writing process my angels *did* consistently confirm that my purpose was to write, but they explained that rather than a mystery, my first published work was meant to be a nonfiction teaching manual to help readers learn to channel. My angels kept insisting, and I demurred because I loved writing the novel. After I finished the book and began the process of manifesting, all I encountered was rejection. I confronted my spirit guides in total frustration, asking for an explanation. They responded by reminding me that they *had*, in fact, spent *three years* plainly telling me that a novel would *not* be my first book in print, but that I had repeatedly dismissed what they were communicating. Of course, I had to admit they were right. I don't think I've ever had a more self-critical moment in my life because I realized that after three years of hard work, I had to completely rethink my career as a writer.

Once I started to pay attention to my real spiritual agenda, things began to move forward faster then I could have imagined. Following the completion of the book, *How to Talk With Your Angels*, I wrote down my intent, and once again began the tedious process of trying to get published. But what a different experience this was! I was finally on the right track in terms of what I was to do and when I was to do it. In no time at all, I was able to secure a wonderful literary agent, who in turn sold the manuscript in a period of several months. In the literary community, that was definitely speedy!

Therefore, if you have discovered your spiritual agenda, and are working to achieve it in the appropriate time frames, things are going to be cooking on four burners! If, however, you can't seem to move your life forward and facilitate what you most desire, you are either on the wrong path, or your timing is off. Do you understand why developing an awareness of your spiritual to-do list and its timing plays such a crucial role in manifesting a better quality of life?

I want to share one additional bit of information about manifesting before we examine how to spread intent out into the universe. In addition to writing your intentions about your spiritual agenda, you can also manifest material goods using the same procedure. You may have heard that if you are truly spiritual, material goods are not to be manifested. This is hogwash! You may employ the process of manifesting at any time for anything you wish.

We are currently existing on the earth's physical plane, and although it is a spiritual boot camp where we are to face challenging adversity, there are facets of life here that can be truly enjoyed and savored. What a waste it would be for you to have lived your life without experiencing the material or physical pleasures exclusively available to you during your earthly lifetimes. It is akin to traveling with your family to a magnificent vacation destination like the Hawaiian island of Kauai, or Florence, Italy, and never leaving your hotel room! What's the point of going in the first place? You can't lose sight of your original intent to explore and widen your horizons. I'm sure you've heard the expression, ''When in Rome, do as the Romans do.''

It is perfectly appropriate to manifest material goods, particularly when the object you are trying to secure will help improve the quality of your life, and allow greater forward movement. I promise that you will not be looked upon as shallow or materialistic by the spiritual beings who work with you. It is spiritually respectable to put out an intent for a material object or desire when you live on a material plane. Material things exist to help us enjoy earthly life!

In essence, what I'm saying is that besides freely appreciating material things, you should venture out from your ''room'' and explore the wonderful phenomenon of having a physical body. Enjoy regularly stimulating your sense of sight, sound, taste, smell, and touch.

For example, I write at home in an office that has a big window overlooking a bricked patio, where I can see a number of large oaks, magnolias, elm, and pine trees. All types of birds are attracted to these trees, and one day I heard a sound that utterly captivated me. It was the melodic cooing of two "love doves," as they're called in the deep south where my husband grew up. Now every day that I write, I put out my intent in the universe for doves to appear and share their exquisite singing with me for inspiration.

Now that you understand the process of manifesting, I'd like to share a method I have found that can create spectacular results. You'll need a notebook and pen to begin this exercise, and I would recommend that you try to set aside several hours to do this important work. We'll be focusing on all the various parts of your life. After you've completed this initial process, spend several minutes each day reviewing your list to decide what you can achieve in regard to your goals *that day*. Remember that most goals are achieved one small step at a time. When you start by taking small steps, your life will immediately begin to move forward with an increasing momentum that you'll find exhilarating! Moreover, once you have successfully achieved one-half to two-thirds of your goals, it's time to go back to the drawing board and add to your original list.

To begin, open your notebook and create five different titled sections.

1. Manifesting for My Personal Life
2. Manifesting for My Professional Life
3. Manifesting for My Health and Well-Being
4. Manifesting for My Spiritual Growth
5. Manifesting for Material Items

We'll explore how you may complete each section later in this chapter. Be certain to allocate a number of pages for each category, because you'll be astonished by how quickly and easily you'll fill a page once you get cranking. After you have divided your notebook into the five sections, make a note of the date at the top of each page. Then choose any section to start, and simply make a list of what you most desire. Be as specific as you can. If you aren't immediately certain about the specifics, then wait until you are.

Try to refrain from stating generalities such as "I want a new job" or "I want to find a soul mate." Your list must be fine-tuned, leaving nothing to chance. For example, let's assume that you need a new car. So you would turn to your Manifesting for Material Items list and enter *new car*. However, you must be more specific. What type of car? What year? What model? What color? What type of interior? When would you like this vehicle? What kind of monthly payments are you most comfortable with? Lastly, perhaps you also need to manifest a small windfall to cover the down payment for the vehicle.

Don't limit your lists because you're influenced by friends or family who regularly tell you that what you want is impossible, or that you're too picky. There *is* no such thing as being too picky! Usually, we're not selective *enough* and that's how we end up unknowingly sabotaging ourselves by creating lives that are empty, unfulfilling and depressing.

As you work on your list, consider what you most dream of, or desire. When I was doing my romantic soulmate list, it turned out to be fifteen pages! One evening I was having dinner with a girlfriend and we were discussing what we were individually trying to manifest. I mentioned that among other things, I wanted a man who was on his spiritual journey and had learned to channel. Her eyes widened, and she suddenly broke out in an uproarious peal of laughter. I asked what she considered so funny, and she replied, "You want a man who can *channel* with *angels*? You *must* be joking! I think we'd be incredibly lucky to find a guy who could communicate with *us*!''

Her remark made me laugh, but it also made me feel depressed. What if she was right? Maybe I *was* being too choosy. However, I chose to remain faithful to my dream. I decided that wanting a man who could understand what I did as a life's work was not asking too much, even if talking with spiritual beings *was* a little out of the mainstream. And following years of manifesting, my future husband came into my office for a private session, and the rest is history! In spite of my issue with impatience, I waited until the man came into my life who fit my specifications. I pat myself on the back every day that I didn't settle for less than I knew would make me truly happy. And don't you settle either! When you're creating your lists, you're actually making decisions that will dictate the whole quality of your future life!

One final note about successful manifesting: Once you know what you want to manifest, have thoroughly communicated your desires with your angels, and have written them down as a list of goals, the manifesting process is complete. Although I suggest you review your list *for a moment* at the start of each new day, it is unnecessary to concentrate so much on your list that it becomes distracting or obsessive.

After you have put the energy of what you want into the universe, it's then time to go about your business and focus on other things. Don't fall into the destructive pattern of being a micromanager. You've asked your angels for help and that's all you need to do. You don't need to bug them about their progress by continually asking, ''But if you're going to help me, how come it *hasn't happened yet*?'' No matter how much you want or need something, force yourself to go on about your business and allow your angels to go about theirs. They know what they're doing. It's their mission to help you accomplish your spiritual agenda. Don't forget that there is perfect timing in the universe. If what you are trying to manifest represents a part of your destiny, rest assured it *is going to happen*. Once you have completed the manifesting process, get off the ways and means committee!

The following suggestions are provided to help you start the outline for your manifesting. Remember to be as specific as you can because these lists are what your angels work from and they take your requests very *literally*. Your angels will not independently include other dynamics on your list beyond what you have asked for.

For example, as you peruse the soul-mate list, you might be surprised that you need to be so thorough as to request that the person you are trying to manifest, among many other things, be single, emotionally available, and have already completed issues such as addiction and abuse. You are likely to *assume* that your angels would *know* that you want someone who is available, isn't a drug addict or an alcoholic, and ready for a heart, mind, body, and soul relationship. You'd be dead wrong. If you don't *ask* for someone who is single, you'll actually be telling them that the person's marital status isn't important to you. If you don't *ask* for someone who has already worked through issues of addiction, you'll be telling your angels that the person's sobriety isn't important to you. Get the picture? When drawing up a manifesting list, be as specific as possible!

As my Mr. Wonderful list continued to grow and expand after each one of my bad dates, it came to include such criteria as: a man who doesn't hunt, has no commitment issues, has resolved any dysfunctional issues with his mother, has a basic understanding of channeling, is unpretentious, doesn't take himself too seriously, can be monogamous, is nonjudgmental, is heterosexual, and likes cats. Without experiencing all those bad dates, these things would never have occurred to me as something to include on my list!

When I first started dating my husband, he unknowingly endeared himself to me because of the way he treated the waitstaff at restaurants we visited for dinner. When I was in college, I worked several summers as a waitress and it was some of the hardest work I've ever done. It never ceases to amaze me how rude and thoughtless people can be when they dine out. It is my philosophy that no one should be allowed to dine in any restaurant until they have waited tables for at least two hours, to more fully understand the difficulty of the job. In any case, whenever Britt and I dined out, and he made any kind of request to the waitstaff, he would preface it with a respectful, "Excuse me, sir, but may I have . . ." or "Excuse me, ma'am, but would you please . . ." Following each meal, in addition to leaving a lavish tip, he would thank the waitperson for the service and attention we'd received. I began to respect him and fall in love because of his generosity and his respect for other people's dignity. I tell you that story to illustrate how significant it is to have a specific understanding of *all* the dynamics that are important to you, so you may include them on your list. Don't be concerned that you're being too picky. Instead, make certain that you're being picky *enough*!

I've included the following examples to help you create a basic manifesting list. Use my suggestions simply as a guide. Your list should reflect your individual priorities.

～⋑ MANIFESTING FOR MY PERSONAL LIFE ⋐〜

What You Want in a Romantic Soul Mate

- Height and body type (list what most appeals to you)
- Skin, hair, and eye color (list what most appeals to you)
- Age (give a range you most desire)
- Sexual preference (opposite sex, same sex)
- Emotional availability
- Single
- Person with no addictions (in regard to smoking, drinking, and drug use)
- Person who is currently working on issues
- Person who is working toward their life's work
- Person who is working on spirituality
- Person who is kind, thoughtful, who will consider the relationship a priority
- Person who is emotionally, spiritually, physically, and financially generous
- Preference for a person with children or without children
- Person who wants (or doesn't want) children in the future
- Preference for a person to be divorced or never married
- Person who will be good to my children and/or my pets
- Person who takes care of his physical health
- Person who can be monogamous
- Person who makes me feel positive emotional and physical chemistry
- Person who is creative, sensitive, spontaneous, intuitive, and emotionally expressive

- Person who is responsible, mature, honest, and sincere
- Person who handles money wisely
- Person who is affectionate
- Level of person's education (your preference)
- Level of person's income (your preference)
- Nature of person's career (your preference)
- Approximate time you'd like to meet this individual

Having a Child
- Your preference in terms of being the biological or adoptive parent
- Time frame in which you'd like to have the child
- Healthy pregnancy
- Child who is eager to return to the earthly plane
- If adopted, age of child
- Child's gender
- Child's health
- Issues you'll be willing to help the child with

Drawing Friends Who are Kindred Spirits
- Your preference (if any) as to the gender of the new friends you'd like to attract into your life
- Age range
- Level of spirituality similar or greater than yours
- Friends who can act as spiritual mentors and confidants
- Friends who will be open, sincere, trustworthy, generous, and affectionate
- Friends who understand an even exchange of energy
- Friends who can recognize and appreciate who and what you are
- Friends who are not criticizing or controlling

- Friends who follow through with their promises and commitments to you
- Friends who limit their complaining about *what is* and take action to create what *could be*
- Friends whose goals and aspirations you can respect
- Period of time you'd like the friendship(s) to continue
- Friends with whom you've had positive past-life experiences
- Friends who are understanding of your spiritual agenda and who are supportive and encouraging
- Friends who can make you feel recharged and good about yourself
- Friends who are excited about your achievements and abundance

Creating Better Relationships With Family Members
- I seek to honor outstanding spiritual contracts with my family members
- I wish for my family members to honor their spiritual contracts with me
- I will respect the choices made by my family members in terms of their lifestyle, philosophies, and spirituality because the decisions are strictly theirs to make without my approval or permission
- I will not be in judgment in regard to a family member's level of enlightenment
- I wish to manifest the same level of tolerance and respect from them
- I wish to resolve dysfunctional issues to allow for a peaceful, harmonious and supportive relationship with family members
- I wish to unobtrusively support and encourage family members to fulfill their spiritual agendas

- If a family member chooses not to resolve an issue with me and I have to remove myself from the relationship, I will remain open to a reunion at the time the family member decides to earnestly begin work on the issue

❧ MANIFESTING FOR MY PROFESSIONAL LIFE ❧

Creating Improvements in Your Existing Career
- I'm going to get a promotion (specify a time frame)
- I'm going to get a raise (specify a time frame)
- My raise will be in the amount of such and such
- I'm going to work with a different boss
- My new boss will like me, and will respect and recognize my contributions
- I will have a boss I can like and respect, and who will mentor me any way he/she can
- I'm going to work with different colleagues
- I will have colleagues who like and respect me
- I will have colleagues I can like and respect
- I'm going to get a transfer (specify a time frame)
- I'm going to work in such and such a department
- I'm going to develop new job skills (name the skills you wish to develop)
- I'm going to get a new job outside my company (specify the time frame)
- I'm going to get such and such a job
- I will earn a better salary (specify the amount you'd like to earn)

Starting Your Own Business
- I'm going to start my own company (specify the time frame)

- My new business will center around such and such a product or service
- I'm going to attract investors to provide seed capital (specify amount of capital you wish for)
- Specify location of new business
- I'm going to hire outgoing, resourceful, hard-working individuals (specify number of employees you expect to hire)
- The business will be a great success and running in the black within six months
- The business will create abundance (specify the level of abundance you wish to develop)
- I wish to run the business without a partner (if that is your desire)
- I wish to attract a partner to me with whom I'd have a solid, stable, trustworthy relationship (if that is your desire)
- I wish to find the best methods to market my new business
- I will have clients who are happy and satisfied with my products/services
- My clients will refer other business to me

🦜 MANIFESTING FOR MY HEALTH AND WELL-BEING 🦜

- I'm going to have the best possible health throughout this lifetime
- My body will attempt to heal any illness or disease that currently exists
- My body will attempt to resist any future health condition

MANIFESTING FOR MY SPIRITUAL GROWTH

- I will stay balanced, centered, calm, and unruffled by other people's issues
- I am not interfering with any other person's spiritual agenda
- I am successfully working through my own issues
- I will stay balanced, centered, calm, and dignified while I work on my own issues
- I will not allow another person to slow down or derail my spiritual growth
- I am developing a tangible relationship with my angels
- I am creating the opportunity to mentor others
- I will accomplish everything on my spiritual agenda for this lifetime
- My soul is providing greater levels of self-awareness
- I am moving toward accomplishing my life's work
- I am attracting soul mates with whom I share my spiritual journey
- I will have vivid dreams about my past lifetimes
- I will develop a remembrance of the heavenly plane
- I will develop an understanding and acceptance that there is perfect timing in the universe so that I may learn to enjoy each and every day of my life's journey

✌ MANIFESTING FOR MATERIAL ITEMS ❧

- I wish to earn additional money from my career
- I wish to move to a larger home (specify where, when, the cost of the home, as well as its physical description)
- I wish to start an art collection (specify type of art, size of collection)
- I wish to retire at such and such an age (specify the time frame and where you will live upon retirement)
- I wish for new furniture, vehicle, vacation, clothes, jewelry, private school for children, etc.
- Specific physical description of above
- I wish for someone to help me with the housework or the children
- Description of help you'd like to receive, and person who would provide it
- I wish for college funds for my children
- I wish for a windfall to pay off my debts (specify time frame)
- I wish for enough abundance to pay for medical expenses

This list is only an outline. Your list will be very personal and reflect your most intimate desires. Don't lose sight of the fact that your manifesting list is a series of goals for you to reach in partnership with your angels. You can carry your end of the apple cart only by way of contributing a significant amount of elbow grease. It does happen that on rare occasions something you are attempting to manifest will immediately fall into your lap, but it's more likely that each and every entry on your list will take some effort on your part. As you manifest and create a partnership between you and your angels, the entire process of physically creating what you most desire will become unbelievably easier.

Don't get frustrated if this exercise takes a little more time than you expected, particularly if you've been singly focused on your past, or haven't ever considered what you most want or acknowledged your ability to manifest. As time goes on and you develop greater wisdom and enlightenment, you'll become much more self-aware, and will consistently have new entries to add to your manifesting list.

For example, I have a client who is a single woman in her thirties who wants to find her romantic soul mate and get (re)married before she reaches menopause. She compiled an exhaustive list of what she wanted in a husband that she believed was fully developed. However, she had a hideous blind date that allowed her to add to her list.

Her companion that evening was thirty minutes late for their date without calling, spoke venomously about his ex-wife, chose a barbecue steakhouse for dinner knowing full well she was a vegetarian, ignored how *she* looked while staring appreciatively at other women, drank excessively, and expected physical intimacy with her that first night. When she refused, he dropped her off at the curb like a hot potato. Following this date, she had more items to add to her soul-mate-manifesting list that would have *never occurred to her* if she hadn't gone on that date. For instance, she added the following.

- A man must be on time or call to let her know he's running late
- A man who understands and respects her revulsion for meat. Perhaps a fellow vegetarian

- A man who refrains from noticeably admiring other women
- A man who recognizes the effort she took to prepare for a date
- A man with no addiction issues
- A man who wants to get to know her emotionally before he makes sexual advances
- A man who is a gentlemanly enough to open her car door, pull out her chair, and pick her up, and drop her off protectively at her front door
- Refrains from talking about ex-wives, girlfriends, lovers, etc. while out with her, particularly on a first date

As your life experiences add to your levels of maturity, you can use this new awareness to build the foundation of what you are specifically manifesting. The next time you have a bad date, a terrible day at the office, a frightful case of the flu, or a significant financial upset, get out your manifesting notebook and add to what you have previously itemized.

And finally, develop a sensitivity toward *how* you ask for what you want. If you say or write, "I *need* such and such," then you will get just what you asked for. You will remain in a state of *need*. If you say or write, "I *want* this or that," then you will again manifest just what you asked for. You will remain in a state of *want*. State your intent to the universe in the most positive and confident language, as if you are fully committed to the process of creating what you most desire and it is already becoming a reality. For instance,

| If you are insecure financially: | "I *have* abundance. And I am creating more abundance every day." |

If you are unsatisfied emotionally:	''I am *definitely* going to meet and marry my soul mate. Each day he draws closer to me.''
If you are floundering professionally:	.''I *am* moving into my life's work. It is totally satisfying and financially rewarding. I picture myself as a success.''

Try to be patient as you work on your ability to manifest. Although some dynamics of your manifesting list will instantly materialize, don't get too accustomed to immediate gratification. Trust that there is perfect timing in the universe, although it may not always mirror the time frame in which you would like to see your intentions become reality.

PART THREE

∽

Your Spiritual Future

EIGHT

Using Timing to Your Advantage

TIMING PLAYS A crucial role in your ability to accomplish your spiritual agenda. Timing may be described as the process of making a decision about where you want to go and how you want to get there, and then following through with the appropriate action on a schedule that will ensure your success.

The speed at which you move forward often determines the success or failure of your career, personal relationships, ability to resolve issues, and even your health. Have you ever found yourself enormously frustrated because you failed to act within a certain period of time, and that hesitation caused you to lose a wonderful opportunity? By contrast, have you experienced the heartache that can result from jumping headlong into a relationship you knew wasn't right because you were lonely and needy, instead of waiting for a person who embodied the qualities of a soul mate? Or perhaps you have been in a long-term relationship with someone who was not moving forward with purposeful momentum toward a commitment, and you wondered, "Why isn't the relationship moving forward? He says he loves me, so what's he waiting for?"

In private sessions, I've had a number of clients who were steadily working toward their spiritual agendas, but who hadn't yet met with the success they anticipated. Discouraged, they would lament, "I'm twenty-nine! [or thirty-nine, forty-nine, fifty-nine, etc.] I thought I'd be so much further ahead by now!" or "Why is it that I'm thirty-five years old, working myself to death, besieged with money problems, living alone in a small apartment with a cat, while my old college girlfriend has a brilliant career, a great husband, two healthy children, a lovely home, trips to Europe, and a perfect body?" or "I'm better at what I do than some of the really successful people out there, so why am I still an unrecognized failure?" or "Most older people my age are retired and enjoying life, and here I am stuck in a menial job with deteriorating health!"

When we find ourselves frustrated because our lives lack stimulating momentum, we often compare what little we have achieved with all the trappings of success that others are enjoying, which makes us feel even worse about our situation. However, when you feel unhappy or distracted because your life is not moving forward with any satisfying momentum, you can rest assured that you *are correct* in your observation. If *you* feel your life is at a standstill, it most certainly *is*. It doesn't matter what other people think about the fact that you should "Be grateful for what you *do* have" or "But at least you have your health!" or "I know a lot of people who would love to have your life! You're just never satisfied!"

Realizing that you are not happy with where you are at the present is actually a very positive discovery. If you are unhappy, it means that there are dynamics of your life that have stagnated and *are not moving forward*. As long as you are involved in working toward achieving your goals, you have something to look forward to. So if you aren't happy, it means you are very likely experiencing one, or a combination, of three things.

First, the problem could be that you haven't yet done your spiritual homework to discover your individual spiritual destiny, and you have no awareness as to what your goals should be. If this is the case, I recommend that you go back and review previous chapters, which will give you a completely different perspective of your life and level of spiritual self-awareness.

Second, the problem could be that a significant person in your life is derailing your progress because they are not resolving their issues or honoring a spiritual contract with you. If this is the case, and you'll certainly know if it is, remember that no matter how much you want to, you simply cannot "help" another person move forward and do the work they are meant to do. Prepare yourself to make a choice if this particular person chooses to remain exactly where he is. You can remain indefinitely in the dysfunctional relationship, which will cause you to give up everything you could have achieved on your spiritual agenda, or you may leave the relationship to pursue your individual destiny. Unfortunately, there is rarely another option.

Third, the problem could be that although you have already developed an awareness of your destiny and are working to fulfill it, your sense of *timing* is off. If this is the case, you simply need to expand your existing awareness of your spiritual to-do list to include the specific *time frames*, or schedule, in which you planned to achieve them. *Timing plays an extremely significant role in your ability to reach success on the earthly plane.*

In this regard, if you deliberately attempt to hasten

your schedule because you're tired of waiting to reach certain goals, you'll discover that you can't force things to move forward before the time is right. You'll find yourself conducting unnecessary busy work that actually *slows* your forward movement. On the other hand, when you attempt to deliberately delay your schedule because you're a procrastinator, or frightened of transition, you'll repeatedly forfeit personal and professional opportunities that could have resulted in greater happiness and contentment.

Equally important in a discussion of timing is to underscore the significance of *balance*. If you have reached a level of enlightenment in which you have developed a fine-tuned sense of balance, it means that you live your life with a secure, calm, inner peace. Balance refers to the ability to resolve issues, work toward your life purpose, and honor spiritual contracts while maintaining a serene state of being. It also refers to the ability to reach all of the goals of your particular destiny respecting the perfect timing of the universe.

On the earthly plane, everything happens with perfect timing. Therefore, if you have a new opportunity presented to you or there is transition going on in your life, whether you expected these things or not, they are happening for your best benefit. You will never be confronted by something until you are ready to handle it. Instead of reacting to new opportunities or transition with negativity, fear, or hesitation, a balanced individual would understand that the event was occurring as a learning experience, which will ultimately help him move forward to a happier place. Of course, being balanced does not mean you are an emotional robot. If something frightening or unfortunate occurs, such as being fired from your job, or your husband deciding to run off to Cancun with the baby-sitter, you wouldn't respond by casually saying, "Oh well, too bad, but it must be happening for my best good. I will remain in a complete state of serenity. What's for dinner?''

It would be unrealistic to expect that even after achieving a certain level of balance you'd be able to respond to situations that are unexpected or upsetting without anxiety. As a human being, you're going to experience an emotional reaction to transition sooner or later. However, when you reach a state of balance, rather than *remaining* negative or upset by what is going on, you can quickly begin to calm yourself. The more you practice being balanced, the more balanced you become. Granted, it is a bit of a challenge, because the only way to build a sense of balance within you is to practice at the time you've had an emotional rug yanked out from under you, or during an episode of stressful transition.

The reason behind developing balance is to lessen the amount of time you spend reacting to stress with draining, depressing, or negative emotions. Even in the best of circumstances on the earthly plane, you're continually being exposed to levels of stress that can have long term effects on your physical and emotional well-being. When you take the time and initiative to learn to respond to the stress in your life in a different, healthier way, you'll find the whole quality of your life improving. Let's learn the process of developing balance by addressing a fictional work-related situation. I recommend that you refer back to this passage the next time you're in a troubling or stressful situation, in either your personal or professional life. By doing so, you'll be able to move through the experience without expending as much of your precious emotional energy.

ᵔᔆ THE FIRST STEP: THE EPISODE OCCURS ᖆ

You have been forced to work overtime, uncompensated, because several of your colleagues have taken lengthy vacations. In spite of your efforts, the boss has been grumbling about your job performance. It has always been obvious he doesn't like you, and the environment has become stressful, leaving you completely drained at the end of each long day. Just a few minutes ago, he called you into his office to complain about your sluggish attitude. In a confrontational manner, the boss indicated that you have not been trying hard enough, and he therefore has decided against giving you the raise and promotion he had promised you last year.

THE SECOND STEP: YOU REACT

No matter how enlightened you are, expect to experience a very significant emotional reaction to such a stressful episode that might feel like a fist in the solar plexus. Of course, the level of stress you feel will be in direct proportion to whatever has occurred. Realistically, there is nothing you can do to avoid the initial anxiety, short of entering complete denial or sinking into a coma. Even if you are a person who keeps his feelings hidden, you will still be very aware of the turmoil.

At this stage, when you're really upset over what has transpired and your brain is racing to consider all the negative ramifications of the situation, it's time for an immediate attitude adjustment. *No matter how bad the situation appears, don't allow yourself to wallow in anger, fear, or suffering!* The more you *think* about it, the worse and more horrific the situation will seem. Remember how self-critical the brain can be, with all of its negative mental chatter?

For instance, if you found yourself in a ghastly situation, would you ask for advice from the most negative, critical, and pessimistic person you knew? Of course you wouldn't! Because after speaking with him, you'd feel the situation was even blacker than it initially appeared and you'd feel that much worse! Tell your brain to turn off and *immediately* proceed to step three.

🐲 THE THIRD STEP: CHOOSE TO START FEELING BETTER 🐲

Although you have asked your brain to turn off, you are still likely to feel absolutely dreadful. You may be in tears or feel furiously angry. Don't expect anything less. Unfortunately, we can't turn our feelings on and off like a light switch. Try to consider how positive it is that you're in touch with your feelings, even if you are frightened to death, or feeling miserably depressed. If you couldn't be in touch with your negative feelings, you couldn't be in touch with the positive ones, either.

At this point, you'll begin the process of trying to balance your feelings. You certainly won't be able to erase what has just occurred, but you'll start to derail the anger and/or depression you are feeling, which will short-circuit the "But-it's-so-unfair, what-did-I-do-to-deserve-this, I'm-feeling-so-sorry-for-myself" blues. You're *entitled* to feel all of those things. But as you develop a sense of balance, you will seek to restore a more peaceful quality of life as soon as possible, no matter *what* has just transpired. It doesn't matter if you've created the negative situation, or if the difficulties have been brought about because of the actions of others. When a person is balanced, he *chooses* to make himself feel better, rather than wallow in despair.

In either case, remember that you can choose to feel better *immediately* after you experience the initial emotional reaction to whatever has occurred. Remaining in a negative or traumatized emotional state is as self-destructive as placing the palm of your hand on a red-hot stove burner and deciding to leave it there. Once your palm is burned, there is nothing you can do to go back in time to erase the injury. The longer you choose to keep your palm on the burner, the more serious the injury becomes. But as soon as you decide to remove your palm from the searing surface, even though it's going to initially hurt like crazy, you're instantly helping yourself embark on the road to recovery. Figuratively speaking, once you *choose* to remove your hand from the red-hot burner, you're ready for the next step in recovering your emotional balance.

⁓ THE FOURTH STEP: REESTABLISHING CONTROL ᧞

The worst possible time to be self-critical is when you're angry or hurting emotionally. You must treat yourself with kindness and gentle encouragement. Acknowledge what you have just experienced and how it has upset your emotional balance.

When we experience any kind of upset, it causes our sense of emotional balance to go haywire, and we feel very *out of control*. No matter how dysfunctional or full of turmoil your life may be, remember that you remain in complete control over how you *react* to what happens to you.

While you have no control whatsoever over the behavior of another adult, you always remain in complete control over what you choose to do with your life. The quality of your life is strictly your responsibility. If you repeatedly find yourself in the same stressful situations, and as a result, you feel you've lost control over your life, it is a good time to take stock and ask yourself if you're finally ready to take your hand off that red-hot burner.

The fastest way I have found to redeem your self-confidence and feel that you are once again in control

of your life is to devote a short period of time immediately following a troubling incident to review your
spiritual destiny. All it takes to recapture a sense of control is your decision not to wallow in your suffering,
followed by a quick review of who you are and what
you are here to do spiritually. To that end, you should
consider the following.

- The nature of your life's work and how you will
  make a difference in other people's lives. This
  will help restore a little of your self-worth and
  self-esteem, and remind you that *you are an important person.*
- If this particular situation reflects one of your
  issues, start working to get it resolved as quickly
  as possible to limit the number of these encounters you will have to endure.
- If this experience involves a spiritual contract
  you have with another individual and reflects one
  of his issues, ask yourself if you are honoring it
  appropriately.
- Acknowledge the *timing* of the situation, and the
  fact that the incident happened at *this* particular
  time for a *very particular reason.* Nothing happens by accident in the universe. What are you
  meant to learn?

🐦 THE FIFTH STEP: REGAINING YOUR BALANCE 🐦

Once you have completed the review of your spiritual
destiny, your soul will begin flooding you with positive
encouragement that will help you start to feel better. The
more difficult the experience, the longer it will take you
to reinstate your sense of balance, or control, over your
life.

It is also important to try to remember your level of enlightenment during negative episodes or encounters. During an argument or confrontation, try to keep your voice modulated, and refrain from name-calling or profanity. I know that other people can make you absolutely nutty at times because they behave in an appalling manner, but you have no control over *them*. You *do* have complete control over what *you* decide to do. If you're balanced and in control, someone else's abusive or childish behavior will not compel you to respond in kind. Even in the worst of circumstances, if you choose to behave at your level of enlightenment, you'll have nothing to be embarrassed about, or apologize for later. People who are balanced and in control behave with inner dignity and self-respect.

Building emotional balance is something that you'll need to practice during troubling periods in your life, especially those involving fearful transition. Rest assured that you'll *never* be confronted with transition before you are ready to deal with it. Without exception, we have to spiritually *earn* new opportunities.

Developing balance in your life is not limited to responding to stress or turmoil. It also refers to your sense of timing in terms of how you pursue your spiritual goals and respond to new opportunities. Creating a sense of balance in your life will allow you to consistently move forward to achieve your goals in a comfortable time frame with unwavering momentum.

As we're discussing the parallels between timing and balanced forward movement, I want to ask you a question. In all honesty, would you describe your sense of timing in regard to decision-making and forward movement as calm, self-possessed, and confident? If not, you may be unknowingly sabotaging your quality of life because one or more of the following personality traits are derailing your momentum.

For instance, when you are faced with transition, or an important decision, do you routinely respond with any of these self-destructive patterns of behavior in an effort to slow down or speed up the time frames involved?

🦅 THE WORRIER 🦅

People who have a tendency to worry are likely to respond to decision-making with a statement such as: "Make an important decision? Oh-oh, I was *worried* about this! What if I can't *make* the decision? What if none of the other employees agrees with my decision? What will happen if my decision causes the company to lose money? What if I make the decision, and I lose my job because of it? What if I can't find another job? How will I support myself? If I lose my job, I'll be broke! If I can't make my car payment, my car will be repossessed! I've never been in such a position! I could be forced to file bankruptcy! Oh, my God! Have I got a headache!"

As a worrier, you're sabotaging the timing of your forward movement with the following behavior.

- You find yourself obsessively worrying about family members, friends, business colleagues, strangers, the state of your finances, your job security, and other aspects of your life.
- When you worry, you work yourself into such a frenzy that it ultimately results in an unpleasant physical condition such as a sick stomach or a headache.
- You allow opportunities to pass you by because you are so consumed by worry.
- You often find yourself worrying about things that are so far in the future that concern over

them in the present is nonsensical. For example, you might spend your precious energy agonizing over whether your newborn baby will be able to secure a scholarship for college tuition, or if your future dream house will be hit by lightning and burn to the ground, or if your new puppy could suffer from blindness when he's elderly.

- You frequently obsess over things that ultimately never happen, or are very unlikely to happen.

⮞ THE NEGATIVE ⮜

People who have a tendency toward negativity are likely to respond to decision-making with a statement such as, "Make an important decision? This is *typical*! My life will *never* change. I'm sure they came to me because no one else wanted to do it! I'll *hate* making this decision. It's nothing but a trap! Someone is trying to make me look foolish. I'll bet they're trying to sabotage my promotion next month. No *wonder* I'm so suspicious of everyone around here!"

By being negative, you're sabotaging the timing of your forward movement with the following behavior.

- Your first reaction to anything unexpected is suspicion or distrust.
- You complain about everything.
- You are often paranoid about other people's motives and intentions.
- You are frequently depressed, sad, or angry.
- You believe that life can be nothing more than one hideous occurrence after another.
- You reject new opportunities because you fail to see them as a positive symbol of forward movement.

- You believe other people who are happy are fooling themselves, or in some kind of dangerous denial.
- No matter how unhappy you are, you don't trust any kind of change because things are only liable to get worse than they already are.

✎ THE FEARFUL ✎

People who have a tendency to be fearful are likely to respond to decision-making with a statement such as, "Make an *important decision*? But I'm not sure what to do! What if my decision is *wrong*? Everyone will criticize me! We shouldn't even make the decision. It will change things and we don't know what the future will bring!"

By being fearful, you're sabotaging the timing of your forward movement with the following behavior.

- You find yourself afraid to make a decision because of possible confrontation from others, and the possibility that you could be *wrong*.
- You hesitate to engage in any forward movement because self-critical mental chatter keeps reminding you of mistakes you've made in the past.
- You are apprehensive that crossing over new thresholds could bring uncertainty or disaster because you have such a fear of the unknown.
- You are scared that forward movement could create a more difficult existence than you have now, so it's better not to take any risks whatsoever.

☜ THE PROCRASTINATOR ☞

People who have a tendency to procrastinate are likely to respond to decision-making with a statement such as, "Make an important decision? What's the *hurry?* You know I don't like to be *rushed.* I'll probably get back to you next week. If not, then you can definitely depend on me next month."

As a procrastinator, you're sabotaging the timing of your forward movement with the following behavior.

- You rarely honor commitments you've made in terms of *when* you promised to complete them.
- You have a to-do list that seems to continually snowball.
- Family, friends, and business colleagues always seem to be pressuring you.
- You never feel an ongoing sense of achievement or accomplishment.
- You routinely lose new opportunities because you procrastinate about making a decision.
- You consistently find yourself fibbing or making excuses in an effort to cover up or justify why you haven't done something.

☜ THE LAZY BONES ☞

People who have a tendency toward laziness are likely to respond to decision-making with a statement such as, "Make an important decision? Why *me?* I made a decision last month. Can't *someone else* make this one?"

By being lazy, you're sabotaging the timing of your forward movement with the following behavior.

- Another person makes a request, no matter how trivial, your first reaction is to somehow weasel out of complying or helping.
- You never seem to honor the promises or commitments you've made to yourself or to others.
- You often feel physically and mentally tired from boredom.
- You have no real initiative to set any goals.
- You find yourself locked in the same dull routine at work.
- You find yourself locked in the same dull routine in your personal life.
- You reject the offer of new opportunities because you dread the thought of additional work or responsibility.
- Although you're exhausted by the same old routine, you rarely do anything new to change your life, including looking for a more satisfying job, making new friends, exploring a new hobby, or even trying new foods.

☙ THE ANAL-RETENTIVE ☙

People who have a tendency to be anal-retentive are likely to respond to decision-making with a statement such as, "Make an important decision? Not so fast! I must weigh and analyze every nuance of the situation because I *won't* move forward until the outcome is *guaranteed*."

By being anal-retentive, you're sabotaging the timing of your forward movement with the following behavior.

- You find spontaneity frivolous.
- To make any kind of decision at all, you find yourself stubbornly analyzing the situation to

death, weighing every option, and exploring every possible negative ramification.

- It is often impossible for you to make a timely decision.
- You have a difficult time moving forward if the results cannot be guaranteed.
- You may have the issue of being commitment-phobic, because you fear being emotionally smothered in a close relationship, or the possibility of a divorce.
- You are often judgmental toward decisions others have made that have turned out badly for them.
- Instead of feeling compassion or sympathy for others in a difficult emotional situation, you feel superior that you haven't made those "mistakes."

❧ THE IMPATIENT ❧

People who have a tendency to be impatient are likely to respond to decision-making with a statement such as, "Make an important decision? No problem! But only *one*? Give me ten minutes! No! I can whiz through it faster than that! Making *any* decision, even if it moves us forward in the *wrong* direction, is still better than hesitating and not moving forward *at all*!"

By being impatient, you're sabotaging the timing of your forward movement with the following behavior.

- You create a life that is one big, mad scramble.
- You are forever complaining that things just don't happen fast enough.
- If things aren't happening fast enough, you cre-

ate unnecessary busy work that serves to complicate your life.

- You begin quite a few projects, but usually have a problem with the follow-through required to actually finish them.
- Although you enjoy the challenge of juggling a number of different tasks at one time, you are often disorganized.
- Instead of waiting for a brief period to consider all of your options, you have developed the habit of leaping into the first opportunity offered to you, regardless of the possible consequences, because it is offered to you *now*.
- You complain about frequently losing or misplacing things.
- When things don't move fast enough, you try to arm-wrestle the universe by attempting to *force* things to happen, which in reality, slows everything down to a crawl until you're back on track.

~ THE OVERCOMMITTED ~

People who have a tendency to be overcommitted are likely to respond to decision-making with a statement such as, "Make an important decision? You came to the right place! I always say, if you want something done, then ask a busy person! I can fit a decision in my schedule tomorrow morning between ten-thirty and ten-forty. No! That's impossible! I have a telephone meeting with the people from Seattle. How about nine-forty-seven on Thursday? No, wait . . . I have a doctor's appointment. How about eight-thirty-five next Tuesday? Oh, that's when I have my time management consultant penciled in. How about six-fifteen on Friday? No, I can't then either . . ."

By being overcommitted, you're sabotaging the timing of your forward movement with the following behavior.

- Your schedule is so jam-packed that you have no freedom.
- You find yourself often falling miserably behind schedule because you plan too much on your daily to-do list.
- You have difficulty saying "no" to people when they make a request, no matter how busy your schedule.
- Family members and friends have to make an appointment to spend time with you.
- You find yourself rushing from task to task, feeling overwhelmed, frustrated, and exhausted.
- You feel depressed and angry with yourself because your life is so centered around tasks, obligations, and responsibilities that you have no time to recharge or have fun.

If you suffer from any of these tendencies, you're dramatically slowing down your forward movement. In essence, what you're doing is *preventing* the opportunity to build a wonderful quality of life because you're *getting in the way.* When you can avoid falling into these negative patterns of behavior, you'll begin to build a natural spiritual and emotional balance which you'll be able to comfortably maintain, no matter what is going on in your life. The more centered and balanced you remain, the *faster* your progress will take place, and the sooner you'll be developing the quality of life you've been dreaming about.

The true measure of balance inspires an unwavering sense of inner power. Your inner power allows you to remain in control of your life, and will fuel all of the forward movement necessary to achieve your spiritual destiny. When you concentrate on your spiritual agenda, you'll help maintain your sense of balance and timing, and you'll discover a new emotional peace and contentment with where you are at the *present*. As you become aware of your destiny and work toward fulfilling it on a daily basis, you'll be creating an inner spark of excitement that will continually give you something to look forward to.

If you have written your list of goals and are doing everything possible to achieve them without trying to force or delay the timing, you'll be experiencing a real sense of achievement and a growing awareness that your current quality of life really isn't as negative, frustrating, or hopeless as you may have believed.

With your goals firmly in mind, you'll be focused each day with a resolute determination to achieve them. You will no longer be reviewing the past and beating yourself up over previous mistakes. Instead, you'll spend your time productively concentrating on the present and the future, and you'll draw other people to you who are doing the same.

Once you experience a tangible sense of accomplishment because you're no longer fighting the timing in which you are to reach your goals, you'll recognize the heady feeling of really being in control of your life.

NINE

❧❧❧

Why Making a Mistake
is Impossible

HOW OFTEN HAVE you looked back and reminisced over particularly painful periods in your life and judged the valuable *lessons* you've encountered as unfortunate *mistakes*? If you've done so, and most of us have, you've probably invested enormous levels of emotional energy berating yourself for your "mistakes."

Are you aware that the fear of *repeating* mistakes can cause you to hesitate in your forward movement, and therefore lose precious opportunities to create a better quality of life? How many times have you thought of a negative episode you've encountered in the past, and repeatedly chastised yourself for creating it? I refer to this self-destructive process as *negative reminiscing*.

For example, if you've gone through a divorce, there are several ways in which to measure what has occurred. You may look upon the entire incident as a fabulous learning experience that you'll never choose to repeat. Or you may choose negative reminiscing, senselessly battering your heart and soul with brutal accusations such as, "How could I have been so *stupid?* I thought I was smarter than that! Why did I stay in the relationship so long? Why did I marry that awful person in the first place? I guess I can't trust my judgment any more. I've wasted so much time! And now I have to start all over! What a terrible mistake I've made!"

No matter what befalls you, you're in complete control of how you measure the experience. For instance, if you have been laid off, you can look upon what has happened as a necessary spiritual lesson that has led you to greater awareness. Or you could berate yourself thinking, "I had the *feeling* that was going to happen! Why didn't I *do* something before they got rid of me? I'm *worthless*! I'll *never* achieve anything! I worked so hard for those people and they never appreciated me! They never paid me what I was worth! All those *years* I wasted on that job! What a terrible mistake to have stayed there!"

Perhaps you've had a love affair that broke your heart, or bought a car that turned out to be a lemon, or secured a home that was of shoddy construction, or used your life savings for a business venture that became insolvent, or loaned money to a friend that was never repaid.

Many people consider a "mistake" as an error in judgment made in a particular situation that (a) initially appeared very positive, but eventually turned out differently, or (b) initially appeared to be very problematic, and eventually turned out exactly as expected.

How could an opportunity that initially appeared so *positive* turn out *badly?* As we've previously discussed, although you have complete control over *your* actions, you have *no* control whatsoever over the actions of the other people in your life. You might have a soul-mate-type of business or personal relationship with an individual who decides to act far beneath his level of enlightenment, which would cause all kinds of unexpected chaos between the two of you. Perhaps *you* may not always behave and respond toward others at *your* existing level of enlightenment, and ultimately become a disappointment to *them*. Or, in certain circumstances, your angels may determine that there is something better for you than what you are currently working toward, and deliberately stymie your progress until you can come to an understanding of the new, bigger opportunity.

By contrast, however, there are times when an individual deliberately decides to launch into an experience that initially, and unmistakably, appears to be problematic. We often make the choice to intentionally move forward into an *expectedly* difficult situation out of loneliness, depression, boredom, hopelessness, or denial. We choose to blithely ignore the red flags that *always* surround unnecessary lessons, and because it is impossible to escape the wretched outcome of such circumstances, we become increasingly angry with ourselves that we were *knowingly* so self-destructive.

In these situations, it's extremely difficult to force oneself to consider the wisdom achieved, and plan to put it to good use the next time such a situation arises. Instead, most of us find it too hard not to succumb to negative reminiscing because, in retrospect, we feel we *deserve* the self-inflicted emotional beating. When we do this, we begin to invalidate our ability to make *any* future decisions. We demand of ourselves over and over again, ''What was I *thinking*? How could I have been so *stupid*? I knew better! I saw those red flags! How could I have ignored them? I guess I'll always be a senseless idiot!''

Have you ever become tired of waiting for your romantic soul mate, and become involved in a relationship with someone you *knew* was clearly not of your caliber? Have you ever invested money in an endeavor that seemed far too good to be true? Have you ever waited too long to search for a job and in the process, gone through all your savings, or run up crushing debt? Have you placed your trust in someone who has a significant history of betraying or hurting others? Have you seen red flags billowing around any kind of situation and moved forward anyway? If you have, you're in very good company!

But those episodes of your life have not been mistakes. You're wasting precious energy by telling yourself that you *failed* in some way, and that you were stupid, naive, or immature to have created the situation in the first place. In reality, those ''mistakes'' were precious learning experiences toward which you gravitated because you needed more work on those particular lessons. By experiencing those lessons, you have built upon your existing levels of wisdom, enlightenment, and maturity. Moreover, you will continue to gravitate toward the lessons that are necessary for you to accomplish your spiritual agenda so that you may have the opportunity to reach the destiny you planned for this lifetime.

Although you are accountable for your behavior, it is very important to understand that your mistakes have been vital lessons that have not slowed down, but instead, actually *accelerated* your forward movement. If you do not allow yourself to participate in learning experiences, then you are not living your life the way you originally intended. If you are not learning, then you are not growing. And if you are not growing, then you are ultimately wasting your life.

Your spiritual goals, however, exclusively center on those learning experiences that you *planned* to encounter. You have the opportunity to avoid the lessons that you've already mastered. At those times when you angrily look inward and ask, ''How could I have been so dumb? I had a feeling from the start that this wasn't going to turn out like I wanted!'' there is a strong possibility that the experience might have represented a lesson that you didn't need to revisit. But since you already *did*, wouldn't it be more constructive to invest your spiritual and emotional energy in telling yourself, "Well, now I really understand that issue! This is one lesson I'm never going to forget!" By being self-supportive, you're recognizing the hurt you suffered and taking full responsibility for your choices, but you're not continually beating yourself up and creating a fear of making future decisions.

Each time you berate yourself over a particular lesson, you'll relive the experience over and over again, creating much more inner turmoil and confusion. In time, reliving those unhappy events will compel you to disregard what your inner voice is attempting to communicate. You'll end up destroying any confidence you had in decision-making. Eventually, this will cause you to close your heart to intimate relationships, make it impossible for you to engage in necessary commitments, to forge trust in others, or to take the crucial risks that will move your life forward in a positive direction.

When you attempt to avoid life's lessons, you limit your ability to take risks in the future, eliminating any chances of developing a happy romantic relationship, and delaying all of the forward movement that would have led to professional achievement and financial abundance. When you succumb to negative reminiscing, you begin to view your mistakes, or lessons, as challenges you wish you never encountered. This is a colossal waste of your time and energy. You become blinded to the fact that no matter how you berate yourself in the present, you can't go back in time and undo a mistake from the past. It has already occurred and there is nothing you can do to alter that reality.

And if you close yourself in a cocoon of self-protectiveness against the possibility of making future mistakes, you're completely shutting down any new growth toward greater wisdom, enlightenment, or maturity. Most important, you're overlooking the *reason* behind why those challenges emerged in the first place.

I'm going to share a universal truth with you about making mistakes. In spiritual reality, it is *impossible to make a mistake*. Therefore, no matter what you have done in the past, you have never made a mistake. Neither have I. Nor have your family or friends, or any other living being since the beginning of time. There is no such thing as a *mistake*. There are only *learning experiences* toward which we gravitate to further boost our existing levels of spiritual awareness.

However negative your particular challenges have been, they were not *mistakes that you should have avoided*. Instead, they were important lessons that were actually a part of your destiny, or you wouldn't have been so inclined to experience them in the first place. Trust in the fact that throughout all of this lifetime, you will never make a mistake. You will, however, be attracted to certain learning experiences that will serve as important lessons for you to build upon your existing levels of enlightenment.

By the time you recognize a situation in your life as one you would describe as a mistake, you've already activated your awareness of the learning process that will steadily direct you to move forward and divest yourself of the negative situation. You've outgrown the lesson. Therefore, when you first sense a relationship is going sour, or you feel a penetrating disillusionment at work, or you know you're ready to move your home environment, or you feel there is an issue that you can't resolve without therapy, it's time to get the ball rolling!

If you're a little frightened of risk or transition, your knee-jerk response to immediate forward movement may very well be, ''Are you *crazy*? The situation will probably get better! It's a *mistake* to act in haste. I'm going to wait and see!"

But what happens when we "wait and see" is that the situation steadily becomes more of a drain, and we feel increasingly depressed and unhappy. By delaying your departure from a life situation you've outgrown, you're needlessly prolonging the lesson.

For example, if you have a spouse who has just become physically abusive for the first time, it is very likely that he or she will continue that behavior. If you've just discovered that your significant other has been unfaithful, it is very likely that he or she will continue that behavior. If you have a boss who has just passed you up for a promotion, it is very likely that he or she will continue to do so. If you learn that your child has just begun to experiment with drugs or alcohol, it is likely that he or she will continue to experiment. If you're feeling lackluster about where you live, it is likely that you'll continue to be dissatisfied with your existing home environment.

When we have these gentle nudges from the universe and an awareness that things are going badly, we're actually getting the message, "It's time to move forward and do something about this! We're already learning the lesson!"

The longer we "wait and see," the worse things generally become, until we feel so despondent we want to throw ourselves in front of a speeding freight train! When we ignore instincts that suggest, "Oh-oh, maybe I should remove myself from this lesson," we are not only hurting ourselves, but may be unknowingly hurting others in the process. Children, in particular, can be devastated by parents who choose to perpetuate their dysfunctional learning experiences with one another, because as dependent youngsters, they have no control over the situation unfolding between the adults in their household.

In this regard, it's actually a triumph when you can look into your past and recognize that it's littered with a large number of learning experiences that you've overcome, which you may have been regarding as your biggest regrets. Those learning experiences have helped you evolve into the person you are today.

The key to transcending the inclination to regard important spiritual *lessons* as senseless *mistakes*, and to shut down the self-critical rhetoric, is to begin objectively assessing the patterns of lessons you've experienced. I have developed a very insightful technique that will help you create what I call your mistake genealogy. I realize that you most likely have a very hectic schedule, but I'm encouraging you to devote some of your time to the written exercises in this book. Each one serves a very different purpose. And rest assured, I would never recommend anything to you that would be a waste of your time or energy.

To compile your mistake genealogy, you'll need a notebook and pen, and a fairly quiet place to work. To begin, open your notebook and write *Personal Mistakes* at the top of the first page. Leave the rest of the page blank. Turn to the next page, and write *Professional Mistakes* at the top of the sheet. Leave the rest of the page blank. Now turn to the next sheet in your notebook, and write *Spiritual Mistakes* at the top of the page. Leave the rest of the page blank. And finally, turn to the next sheet, and at the top of the page, enter *Health Mistakes*. You now have four separate pages in your notebook prepared with the aforementioned titles.

The next part of the project involves thinking back to the period in which you first began to make your own adult, independent decisions. The age at which we usually start to make adult decisions is different for each of us, but for most people, it's usually sometime in our teens.

Turn to the page titled *Personal Mistakes*, and concentrate on troubling episodes that you have considered mistakes in your personal life. You must begin at the time in your life when you first began to make your own decisions because your mistake genealogy is not supposed to reflect the decisions of your parents or any other adult that were forced upon you. Your list will exclusively reflect only those decisions that were yours alone. Develop your list as fully as you can, right up to the present. Your entries may look something like this.

- I was mean to a high school sweetheart when I . . .
- I repeatedly lied to my parents when I told them . . .
- It was a mistake to turn down that scholarship to XYZ University because . . .
- It was a mistake to keep changing my major in college because . . .
- It was a mistake not to choose to go to college because . . .
- It was a mistake to be physically intimate with so-and-so because . . .
- It was a mistake to marry so-and-so because . . .
- It was a mistake not to have been a better parent to my child because I . . .
- It was a mistake to have remained in the marriage to so-and-so because . . .
- It was a mistake to have cheated on my spouse because . . .

These entries are just examples of what you may choose to include on your list. If you really put some

elbow grease into this exe*
quite exhaustive and lengthy. *
you're compiling a chronological lis*
have already successfully completed.

While you are working on this project, *as*
yourself to get caught up in more negative remin
Don't expend any more of your precious time or energ
beating yourself up. In my way of thinking, you'd only
have something to worry about if you had *nothing to
include* on your list! All of your entries represent hard-
earned wisdom and enlightenment. The greater number
of lessons behind you, the fewer you'll be forced to encounter in the future.

Once you feel you have completed your *Personal
Mistakes* page, you'll turn to the other three pages and
follow the same format. Each of your lists will probably
be enormous, but this is a positive sign that you are
moving forward. These lessons are all *behind* you.

After you've completed making your list of mistakes,
ask yourself the following questions.

- Why did I consider this a mistake?
- What was the lesson I was supposed to learn?
- Was this a necessary lesson, or a repeat of a
  lesson I had already outgrown?
- When do I remember realizing that it was a mis-
  take?
- After I discovered my mistake, how did I react?
- How quickly did I react?
- If I didn't immediately react, but instead as-
  sumed a "wait and see" attitude, why did I
  choose to do that?
- When I did react, how did my quality of life
  change for the better?
- As I create this list, do I recognize a pattern of
  having repeated the same mistakes?

different
ay have I
son?

I would de-
n to do about

the situation?
of life changing
to react and choose

cise, expect your list to be
of the lessons you
This is good! Remember,
not allow
stressing

195

When y   st of mistakes, remember
that there are   n the universe. Everything
that happens throug   ur life has occurred to help
you accomplish your spiritual agenda. Each mistake, or
lesson you have encountered, has heightened your level
of self-awareness, which has helped to reinforce your
existing foundation of inner strength.

The last part of this exercise involves a statement that
you will make to yourself with all the gentleness and
sincerity you can muster. I strongly recommend you say
the following aloud.

"I acknowledge all of these mistakes as lessons I
needed to learn from. I recognize that participating in all
of these lessons has helped me build upon my foundation
of wisdom and enlightenment. Because of these lessons,
I am a much more mature and spiritual person. I will
not revisit any of the lessons that I have already outgrown. I now give myself permission to let the lessons
go. I will never critically mention them to myself again,
except to happily reflect that they are in my past. I now
live every day in the present. I will also have faith that
my future will be filled with limitless opportunities. I
value all the painful work I've done. I'm moving forward daily to accomplish my spiritual agenda. Thank
you, self, for working so hard."

As your life continues to unfold and you're faced with new and different lessons, try to acknowledge them as positive signs of spiritual growth. They are a sure indication that your life is truly moving forward!

TEN

❧❦❧

Avoiding the Quicksand
of Inertia

AS WE EMBARK on the final leg of our journey together, I want to make sure you are completely aware of the power you have to fully control your emotional and spiritual well-being.

Like the physical body, the heart and soul can wither and weaken from self-abuse and neglect. But unlike the physical body, you will *never*, in *any* of your lifetimes on earth, experience a wasting condition of the emotions or spirit that you cannot overcome.

While it is true that you have the ability to heal your emotional and spiritual self, it is essential that you understand the importance of preventive maintenance. But how do you protect your heart and soul in order to maintain good emotional and spiritual health? You must avoid the quicksand of inertia.

Inertia is a human condition more demoralizing and masochistic than any other. If you suffer the malady of inertia, you will never successfully achieve your spiritual agenda, and will instead live your life feeling as if you were a prisoner hopelessly locked inside a cramped, darkened cell.

Inertia begins like a tiny but virulent form of emotional cancer. If left unchecked, it can swiftly grow into a tangled web of despair that can wrap itself around the heart, where it steadily suffocates joy and optimism. It will continue to spread its decay, finally engulfing the soul, where it does its most deadly damage by corroding, and finally extinguishing, faith and spiritual awareness.

Inertia is the state in which an individual fully realizes that he is truly miserable and unsatisfied, yet *chooses to do nothing*. The ravages of inertia become more profound and intolerable as time goes by, leading to feelings of desperation, inadequacy, and depression.

An individual who experiences inertia feels an overwhelming disparity between where he *is* and where he would *like to be*. His hopelessness and poor self-esteem keep him from setting goals and from acting in ways that could change his life for the better. He may spend an inordinate amount of time daydreaming about who or what he could be, if only . . .

In order to cope with the emotional suffering he incurs from not following his spiritual agenda, he often builds a wall of complacency around him in order to make his mediocre existence bearable. Hiding behind this wall is the only way he can continue to tolerate unacceptable behavior from others, boredom with a lackluster daily routine, financial insecurity, and the sense that no matter how long he lives, his life will never change. He increasingly doubts that he will ever have the power to expand the quality of his life beyond its current narrow boundaries.

However, inertia cannot begin to assault your spirit if you *acknowledge* a learning experience that you find hurtful, worrisome, or distracting. Truthfully acknowledging difficult situations helps you evolve into a more enlightened being. Inertia can only invade your heart and soul when you *accept living with the difficulty indefinitely*, denying that it has any real impact on your peace of mind, sanctity of spirit, or quality of life.

For example, if you build a wall of complacency and decide to remain in a relationship with someone who is verbally abusive, you're going to suffer the terrible consequences, namely the continual shredding of your self-worth and self-esteem. The longer you hide behind your complacency, denying how bad things really are, the worse the situation will become. Your level of confidence in your ability to go it alone will continue to plummet as the abuse eats away at your self-esteem. You'll become even more miserable as you see life passing you by while you sit deadlocked in a stupor of inertia.

Similarly, if you build a wall of complacency and decide to remain in a relationship with someone who is not trustworthy or faithful, you'll be repeatedly hurt, confused, and disillusioned. None of your needs will be satisfied because you're the one doing all the giving, while the other person is doing all the taking. Your relationship will never reflect an even exchange of energy. No matter how hard you work at making the other person happy, or attempting to seek their appreciation, the more likely you'll feel like a hamster on a tread wheel. You'll be working yourself to death, but you won't be accomplishing anything. The longer you choose to ignore how bad things really are, the more you'll feel emotionally and spiritually disenfranchised. You'll eventually realize that the more energy you invest in the relationship, the more your partner distances himself from you.

At the same time, if you build a wall of complacency and decide to remain in a dead-end job, you'll experience a mounting insecurity over your finances, as well as a growing concern that perhaps you lack the ability to secure another job, or perform in a greater job capacity. By staying in this situation, you'll ensure that you'll live the rest of your life from paycheck to paycheck, bored to tears because you'll continue to do the very same job, in the very same environment, with the very same people. The longer you choose to ignore how bad things really are, the more you'll feel that your life has no purpose, and that you're simply surviving.

Do you understand how complacency can evolve into full-fledged inertia? There are times when all of us sink into a period of inertia because of fear, despair, procrastination, or even laziness. If you currently find yourself suffering from inertia in any part of your life, take heart. There is hope! Don't forget that your own soul is already programmed with the awareness of your spiritual destiny, and the time frames in which you are meant to achieve your agenda. And as we've already discussed, you have the power to access that information whenever you choose to start moving forward again.

Remember that at the time you *acknowledge* a situation as being troublesome, you're already close to having outgrown the learning experience. When you feel stuck in a difficult situation and it becomes too frightening or exhausting to move forward, you'll know you're not following your spiritual agenda. When you are failing to stay on track spiritually, the telltale signs will include feelings of increasing unhappiness and dissatisfaction, because it will appear your life has no purpose or meaning, and that you are going nowhere.

By choosing to remain indefinitely in a situation you've clearly outgrown, you'll be forced to accept whatever treatment you receive. In doing so, you'll continue to lower your personal standards in regard to who you are, what kind of life you deserve, and where you are going.

Therefore, if you consider the current quality of your

life, and determine that you have outgrown a relation-ship, or your job, this is a real time to celebrate! Your acknowledgment of inertia can be the fuel that helps you get moving again toward accomplishing your spiritual agenda. I realize that considering any kind of life change can be a scary undertaking, but consider your options.

When you're in the process of debating what you're going to do about the parts of your life that are no longer satisfying, ask yourself a question. What is the personal cost you'll have to pay if you remain in the situation you've already outgrown, and what is the personal cost you'll have to pay if you move on with your life? Which choice would cost you more dearly, emotionally and spiritually? Consider the fact that if you get your life moving forward, even if you begin by taking the tiniest of steps, you have nowhere to go but up! And you'll have everything in the world to look forward to.

Regardless of the current status of your life, you have within you an intuitive sense of the standards you should set for yourself, and the scope of the goals you should be striving toward. There is no such thing as delusions of grandeur on the earthly plane. Whatever you desire to accomplish, you may, provided that your goals are a part of your spiritual agenda.

However, when you accept a quality of life *beneath* what your destiny dictates, your soul will consistently tell you that you *deserve a much better existence*. Your effort to deny these intuitive feelings is counterproduc-tive and will make you feel increasingly uncomfortable, and your spiritual and emotional health may begin to suffer.

If you choose to exist indefinitely behind a wall of complacency and remain in an intolerable situation, you will lose sight of how bad the situation really is and will stifle the inner awareness that keeps telling you that you deserve more in your life. You will be giving up pieces of your identity until you have no clue as to who you are anymore.

Moreover, if you then determine that the only way in which you may remain in your existing life is to *continually lower* your standards, before long you will have forgotten all about the earlier awareness of where you were going with your life, and all the wonderful things you intended to achieve.

Once an individual chooses to retreat from life's difficulties behind a wall of complacency and ultimately ignore the assaults on his psyche, he is, in essence, living on emotional and spiritual automatic pilot. No matter what happens to him, he will be accepting, long since having learned to lick his wounds behind his own private wall of hopelessness.

Episodes of inertia are always *self-inflicted*. You can't blame anyone else for the choices you've made that have created your current quality of life. I'm sharing this with you to help you recognize that in order to begin moving forward, you must take full responsibility for the decisions you make. Have you ever found yourself blaming others for your decision to remain in a draining personal or professional situation by declaring one of the following?

- My significant other won't let me leave the relationship.
- My significant other wouldn't like it if I got another job.
- My significant other doesn't want me to work.
- My significant other insists on handling all the money.
- I can't do such and such because of the kids.
- My kids wouldn't accept me going out with a friend, or developing a hobby that didn't include them.

- My family has always expected me to do this, so I can't disappoint them.
- My family knows what is best for me.
- I have to put up with Gladys because she's the only friend I have.
- My boss doesn't want me to leave.
- My boss won't give me a promotion or a raise.
- My coworkers depend on me.
- I can't learn to talk with my soul, or my angels, because my family/friends don't believe it's possible.

When we enter a state of inertia, our mounting unhappiness causes us to blame others for our own lack of initiative. When you're in denial, you cannot accept responsibility for your actions, no matter how dissatisfied you are with your life, because you will continue to deny that you are doing anything that is sabotaging or self-destructive.

After all, you argue, it's not *you* that's causing the problem, it's your parents, your spouse, your kids, your in-laws, your siblings, your friends, your boss, or your coworkers who make it impossible for you to assume responsibility and move forward to improve the quality of your life. If only it wasn't for their demands, needs, and expectations, you could do what you really wanted right now.

If you can relate to these examples of inertia, *this is the time* for you to reassume your personal power and move forward toward your spiritual destiny. Rest assured that inertia is something from which you can always recover, no matter how long the condition has existed. When you've reached the point of being so miserable with your current existence that you can't stand it any longer, you're ready to take responsibility and act as your own spiritual healer.

The antidote for inertia is slow and steady forward movement. You'll begin to feel those walls of complacency coming down brick by brick as you put one foot in front of the other. The first step in tearing down the wall is to quit blaming others and begin to reestablish control over your life. Consider how you can build a stronger sense of personal power by repeating the following.

- I have the power to move my life in a positive direction.
- I have the spiritual awareness that will appropriately direct my forward movement.
- I have the ability to reach unlimited success.
- I do not need anyone's support in order to build a better quality of life.
- I do not need anyone's approval in order to change my life.
- I will expect some resistance from those people in my life who are not ready for this change in me, no matter how positive it is.
- I will not expect the people in my life to immediately recognize the benefits of my forward movement, no matter how obvious it appears to me.
- I will expect that when I take charge of my life, my new initiative will inspire some fear and negativity from those close to me.
- I am the only one who knows what is best for me.
- I am the only one who knows if I am happy with the quality of my life.
- I am the only one who knows when I need to transition out of situations I have outgrown.
- I do not need to make excuses or justify my decisions to those who cannot accept my choices.

- I will understand that if certain people close to me do not accept my decisions, their response to my new initiative is *their choice,* and there is nothing I should try to do to convince them otherwise.
- I will be good to myself by refraining from being self-critical, negative, or pessimistic.
- I need only my own inner support and encouragement to successfully move forward and achieve my spiritual destiny.
- Although at first it may be difficult to change my life and reassert my initiative, I will have faith that things will get easier each day.
- I will have faith that as I persevere, my life will get happier, more secure, and I will feel a very tangible, important sense of purpose.
- I will recognize and support the efforts others are making to accomplish their destiny.
- I will surround myself with people who place a priority on spiritual growth.

At this moment, you have the ability to discover your destiny, and get your life fully on track and moving forward with a purposeful momentum. By doing so, you'll make the most out of this earthly vacation, and create the quality of life that you deserve. Don't limit the scope of what you can accomplish because others around you have far less lofty aspirations. You must be your own person, and wear blinders if you must in order to stay focused on your individual spiritual agenda. If you continue putting one foot in front of the other, particularly when times get tough, you'll prevail to accomplish your innermost dreams and desires. Celebrate the individuality of your soul by honoring what you have come here in this lifetime to do.

I've enjoyed sharing this very special spiritual journey

with you. We've journeyed to the heavenly plane together. We then returned to the earthly plane with an understanding of how we choose our destiny, and how difficult life on the earthly plane can be. You have a new awareness of how your life's work, issues, health, spiritual contracts, and past lives form the important dynamics of your destiny. You have a new ability to access information from your soul's memory bank, and you've learned to use that spiritual awareness to develop more appropriate and satisfying directions for the future. You've discovered how manifesting can tangibly support your forward movement, and how you can reinforce your resolve to continue with your spiritual growth even if you find yourself currently living deadlocked in inertia.

I applaud all your hard work! You are now fully prepared for the future, and I'll be there with you in spirit, as you take each step of your journey. It is now time for you to advance to a higher purpose and accomplish the important mission you have chosen for this lifetime. You're ready to meet your destiny.

ELEVEN

Questions and Answers

THE LAST CHAPTER addresses some of the most popular questions that I have been asked in private sessions, in seminars, and during radio and television appearances. I hope you find them fascinating and informative!

QUESTION: How can I build my intuitive ability to receive information like you do?

ANSWER: Building your intuition is one of the *easiest* things you can do! Every human being on the planet has at least two guardian angels assigned to him to help him achieve his spiritual agenda, and in the process, build a wonderful quality of life. From the time of your birth, you've possessed the ability to communicate with spiritual beings that include your guardian angels, as well as "deceased" friends and family members. The process of communicating with spiritual beings is called channeling. If you're an adult, you've probably long since learned to block your channeling ability in order to be accepted by

other people \
confines of thei
your ability to ch
a little practice. Y
simply because you
neling ability is com
acknowledge them or
remained right at your
from the heavenly plane
protect, and counsel you 1
earth. Therefore, all you ha
communication with them is
by step technique that will have you channeling in no
time! First, you have to acknowledge the fact that you
do have angels who work directly with you. Second,
you need to begin building confidence that you can
receive information from them on your own, and
you'll steadily develop this confidence as you continue to practice. To open up a conversation with your
angels, get a notebook and pen and write several
questions that represent priorities to you. For example, you might ask about the status of a relationship,
or your career, or your health. Ask a specific question,
such as, ''Is my current job secure?'' or ''Is my relationship with Joe going to have a future?'' After
you have written several questions, it's time to call
your angels and start the process of channeling. Say
aloud, ''I wish to speak with my angels. This is my
first question.'' Then ask your question aloud. Within
ten to fifteen seconds, you'll have a telepathic response. This means you'll hear their answer inside
your head, and it will feel exactly as if you are talking
to yourself. Make a note of the angelic information
you hear, and continue to the next question. If, however, you hear nothing in response to your first question, ask another. If you still hear nothing within ten

...scontinue your channeling prac-
...ays. You'll be happy to learn that in
...ce, most people are successful in com-
...ng with their angels very quickly. If you truly
...re to channel with spiritual beings, you have to
remember to practice, practice, practice!

QUESTION: How can my angels help me to accomplish
my destiny?

ANSWER: To receive information about your specific
destiny, you have two options. You may access the
wealth of information stored within your soul's memory bank, or you may ask your angels to provide you
with guidance and direction. If you learn to develop
your channeling ability, it will be incredibly easy to
chat with your angels about what your purpose is for
this lifetime, how you may achieve it, and the necessary time frames in which you need to get it all
accomplished. Any time you feel confused or frustrated, all you have to do is ask for angelic guidance,
and all the answers you need will be immediately
forthcoming. Your angels' entire mission is to help
you achieve your destiny. By taking advantage of
their unwavering help and support, you'll have the
ability to sidestep unnecessary stumbling blocks,
build better relationships, create far greater financial
abundance, discover the reasons behind important
learning experiences, and continue to build a more
powerful momentum in fulfilling your life's purpose.

QUESTION: How can I move forward and change my life
if my spouse and/or other important people are not
supportive of my doing so?

ANSWER: This is a very difficult situation that will probably result in a great deal of soul-searching for you.
You must ask yourself if you really *need* anyone

else's permission, support, or approval to start your journey toward greater spiritual enlightenment. The problem you'll run into is that if you choose to buckle under and do what other people want you to do, you'll become increasingly miserable until you absolutely hate your life, and feel you have no real purpose or direction. On the other hand, if you choose to follow the path toward your life's work, and attempt to accomplish all the other dynamics of your spiritual agenda, you'll end up alienating those people closest to you, especially if they are fearful about forward movement. Quite often, relationships splinter because one spouse, or friend, has decided to embark on his journey, and the other person chooses to remain spiritually stagnant.

QUESTION: Why does my forward movement inspire such negative reactions from those closest to me, when all I'm trying to do is develop greater spiritual wisdom and enlightenment?

ANSWER: Most people remain very negative about *any* kind of change. Moreover, if a person has issues that make him fearful about taking risks or dealing with transition, his response to your forward movement will be negative. As you continue on the path toward your life's work, and as you resolve your issues, you will be creating greater spiritual self-awareness along the way. You will also be steadily enhancing your levels of confidence, and becoming more aware of the caliber of people you want to have in your life, seeking out people who are actively doing the same kind of spiritual work. *You will be changing and evolving*, and this burgeoning enlightenment will be unmistakable to everyone around you. Those who are not quite ready to move forward will be most fearful of your leaving them behind as you continue to travel your chosen path. Unfortunately, as you persevere, and the other person stays exactly where he is, there *will* be an increasing disparity between the two of you. This is how many relationships disintegrate. One person decides to make something more of his life, and the other partner is not ready to start his own forward movement. Rather than being *inspired* by his ambitious partner, the partner who decides to remain in place will soon become angry and resentful if his significant other doesn't quickly abandon all forward movement, no matter how unfulfilling or empty their current existence.

QUESTION: I have already started on my path to greater spiritual awareness. I am reading books, attending seminars, and doing everything I can to promote a better quality of spiritual life. My partner, however, is very skeptical about the things I am doing. What can I do to encourage him to begin his spiritual journey?

ANSWER: Congratulations on your hard work! In regard to your partner, it is important to remember that *he* must want to begin his journey of self-awareness, just like you did. Because you have explored various spiritual venues, you could certainly offer him the books you enjoyed reading, or suggest the two of you take a seminar together. If he declines, for whatever reason, I strongly suggest you *drop the whole subject*. Each one of us must be *independently* fueled by an inner passion to reach our spiritual goals. We can't inspire, convince, or insist that another person begin his spiritual work. To do so would indicate that you have control issues, that you are acting like a spiritual busybody. All you can do is to continue your forward movement and focus on what *you* are trying to achieve. I have learned that the more we attempt to inspire'' a reluctant person, the more likely we are to motivate him to bolt in the opposite direction!

QUESTION: How can I stay focused on my spiritual goals during times of tremendous stress?

ANSWER: It will help if you begin to understand that when you are experiencing a great deal of stress, you are actually in the midst of one or more learning experiences that will allow you to begin another chapter of your life. This is a very positive process because once you've completed the issue(s) that are responsible for causing the stress, you'll enjoy much greater enlightenment, which always translates into a happier and more satisfying existence. However, if you're encountering a great deal of stress in the present, it's hard to focus on a more positive future. Stress is probably causing you to lose sleep, interrupting your ability to focus on your daily routine, inspiring you to eat too little or too much, making you feel cranky or moody, and maybe even causing worrisome anxiety attacks. In addition, if you describe the stress you're experiencing as ''tremendous,'' it's typically a situation that won't be quickly resolved. But there are several things you can do to immediately decrease the sever-

---

When you begin to compile your list of mistakes, remember that there are no accidents in the universe. Everything that happens throughout your life has occurred to help you accomplish your spiritual agenda. Each mistake, or lesson you have encountered, has heightened your level of self-awareness, which has helped to reinforce your existing foundation of inner strength.

The last part of this exercise involves a statement that you will make to yourself with all the gentleness and sincerity you can muster. I strongly recommend you say the following aloud.

''I acknowledge all of these mistakes as lessons I needed to learn from. I recognize that participating in all of these lessons has helped me build upon my foundation of wisdom and enlightenment. Because of these lessons, I am a much more mature and spiritual person. I will not revisit any of the lessons that I have already outgrown. I now give myself permission to let the lessons go. I will never critically mention them to myself again, except to happily reflect that they are in my past. I now live every day in the present. I will also have faith that my future will be filled with limitless opportunities. I value all the painful work I've done. I'm moving forward daily to accomplish my spiritual agenda. Thank you, self, for working so hard.''

will remain centered on your *future purpose*. By concentrating on your purpose, you'll continue living not only in the present, but in the future as well. If you devote half of your energy to envisioning yourself as successful and satisfied in the future, you will have far less energy to devote to what is occurring in the present. Spend some time carefully writing down your spiritual goals as you know them. By doing so, you'll be able to refer to your list at times when you feel like throwing yourself off the top of a very tall building. You'll be amazed at how reassuring it is to review a list of goals that reflect all the wonderful things you are working toward. It will help take the edge off your stress because the list will remind you that you *are* moving forward to create a better life for yourself. You have the ability to overcome anything that is occurring in your life by focusing on your spiritual goals, rather than on the situation that is causing all the stress. By doing so, you'll begin to recognize your life is *still moving forward*.

QUESTION: What do you mean when you talk about battery recharging?

ANSWER: You have four distinctly different batteries that govern the level of energy you have at your disposal. There is the spiritual battery, which provides the "juice" that enables you to channel and access information from your soul. There is the emotional battery, which provides the "juice" for your ability to be creative, sensitive, expressive, as well as to feel positive, optimistic, balanced, and happy. There is the mental battery, which provides the "juice" for your ability to think, reason, focus, and remain alert. And finally, there is the physical battery, which provides the "juice" for your physical body to fight disease, and to allow you a high degree of energy and vitality

elbow grease into this exe...
quite exhaustive and lengthy. ...
you're compiling a chronological lis...
have already successfully completed.

While you are working on this project, *do...
yourself to get caught up in more negative remin...
Don't expend any more of your precious time or energ...
beating yourself up. In my way of thinking, you'd only
have something to worry about if you had *nothing to*
include on your list! All of yo...
earned wisdom and enlighten...
of lessons behind you, the fe...
counter in the future.

Once you feel you hav...
Mistakes page, you'll turn ...
follow the same format. E...
be enormous, but this is ...
moving forward. These l...

After you've complet...
ask yourself the followi...

- Why did I consid...
- What was the le...
- Was this a nec...
  lesson I had al...
- When do I ren...
  take?
- After I disco...
- How quickl...
- If I didn't ...
  sumed a ...
  choose to ...
- When I ...
  change for the bette...
- As I create this list, do I rec...
  having repeated the same mistakes?

with which to carry on all of the daily activities you have planned. At those times when your life is busier than usual, you'll expend more of the juice in your batteries. For instance, if you were to move to another home, you would invest an enormous amount of additional physical energy in the process. If you were studying for an important final exam, or responsible for a major project at work, you would utilize heightened levels of mental energy. If you were to do a great deal of channeling, you would drain your spiritual battery. There is nothing wrong with draining the stockpiled juice from your batteries when you need greater levels of energy. That's what it's there for! However, when you sense that any of your batteries are really becoming drained, you must remember to charge them up again and begin the process of stockpiling new levels of juice.

QUESTION: How do I know when any of my batteries are becoming drained?

ANSWER: It'll be obvious to you when the juice in your batteries starts to dwindle. For instance, if you drain your physical battery, you'll feel exhausted. If enough time goes by and you haven't gone about the business of recharging, you'll come down with an ailment such as a bad cold or the flu, which is your body's way of *forcing* you to rest and recharge. If you drain your mental battery, you won't be able to focus on or comprehend anything. If your spiritual battery is low on juice, you won't be able to channel or access any meaningful intuitive information. And if your emotional battery gets low, you'll feel depressed and negative, and you'll likely find yourself in tears over the most trivial of frustrations.

QUESTION: How can I recharge my batteries when I feel they're getting low on energy?

ANSWER: Recharging your batteries is very simple, as long as you bear in mind that the more depleted your batteries become, the longer it will take for them to restore normal levels of juice. Therefore, you must develop a sensitivity to the levels of juice in your batteries, so that you may begin the recharging process *before* they become completely drained and affect the quality of your life. It is fascinating to note that one or two of your batteries may be running low, but the others may still be going strong. For example, when I leave my office after channeling for clients all day, I like to go to the gym for some strenuous physical exercise. Although my spiritual battery is completely drained, my physical battery is still teeming with energy. However, if you allow any of your batteries to really lose all of their juice, they will start draining the energy out of another battery to continue to operate. Therefore, if you feel emotionally, mentally, physically, *and* spiritually exhausted, you're really in bad shape. What's happened is that you've allowed *all* of your batteries to drain themselves of the energy you need to productively carry on with your life. But now that you know this, you can do something about it! You may be interested to learn that the spiritual, mental, and physical batteries all have the ability to recharge on their own. If you rest the physical body and refrain from physical activity, your body will get the relaxation it needs to renew its stockpile of juice. Sleeping, reading, watching television, snoozing on the couch, taking vitamins, eating healthy foods, and getting a massage are wonderful ways to support your physical body as it recharges itself. You'll know that the physical battery is recharged because you'll feel your energy and vitality returning. Although you'd have to spend an inordinate amount of time channeling to deplete your spiritual battery, once you refrain from channeling or attempting to access information from your soul's memory bank, your spiritual battery will recharge itself beautifully, usually within twenty-four hours. Besides refraining from channeling, there is essentially nothing else you can really do to assist your spiritual battery as it recharges itself. Similarly, when you find it increasingly difficult to concentrate on a mental task, like completing a project for work or balancing the checkbook, and you recognize that your mental battery is spent, it is important to immediately rest your mind by refocusing on a more frivolous pursuit, and your battery will begin to recharge itself. To rest my mind, I enjoy reading a magazine, going to a movie, working out, or having some romantic time with my husband. The emotional battery, however, is different from all of its counterparts because it *does not* have the ability to recharge on its own. You must consistently work to recharge this battery by participating in things that you find emotionally satisfying. The more unfulfilling your life is at the moment, the more time you have to spend in emotional recharging. Because it was ten years between my divorce and the time Mr. Wonderful came into my life, I had to work like crazy to keep my emotional battery recharged. As a single girl, I went out to dinner with friends and family, saw quite a few movies, read stimulating books, bought myself flowers, took bubble baths, got facials, changed my hair color, concentrated on my writing, and ate what I would describe as comfort foods that I "needed" at the time. In addition, I learned the hard way that if I dated men who I knew were not what I was looking for, my poor little emotional battery would be so drained at the end of a miserable date that it would take days of recharging to feel better. If you're single and long to be in a committed relationship, or if you are currently suffering a bad relationship, you'll have to work even harder to recharge, because the emotional battery will be constantly drained due to the loneliness, emptiness, and lack of affection in your life. The harder you work to recharge yourself, the better you'll feel. You may not presently have the personal life that you dream about, but you can make the most of this part of your life by planning fun activities that you look forward to. If you don't do it, no one else will! You'll know that your emotional battery is recharged when you feel more optimistic, happy, and positive about what you're experiencing in the present, as well as a heightened level of confidence about your future.

QUESTION: Do my dreams have a purpose?

ANSWER: Dreams occur for a number of reasons. Most often, they are opportunities for your soul to provide you with intuitive information stored in its memory bank. In some of your dreams, you'll recall a past lifetime, or receive clairvoyant messages about your existing life that are meant to help you work through a particularly difficult problem and aid your forward movement. At other times, you may be visited by spiritual beings that include angels, and deceased family members and friends who wish to communicate with you while you sleep. The reason you receive intuitive information in your dreams is because while you sleep, you are not distracted by all of the outside stimuli that bombards you during waking hours. While it is true that at times the brain releases a flood of negative, fear-based, mental images that represent issues you're working to resolve, most often it is purely intuitive information you are receiving through your dreams.

QUESTION: How can I learn to better interpret my dreams?

ANSWER: In your dreams, you receive two different kinds of intuitive information. First, you have dreams that present literal information that is exactly as you "see" it in your mind's eye. For example, in a dream you might "see" your boss giving you a raise, or "see" your telephone ringing because an old high school friend is calling. Those dreams are exactly what they appear to be and no interpretation is necessary. The second kind of dream is more symbolic, because it provides information that is not readily understandable, compelling you to work to interpret what the dream is meant to convey. In a symbolic dream, you might "see" a butterfly floating across a field of wild flowers, and then the dream might take you to a city street where you are surrounded by noisy traffic. Initially, this dream may not make sense to you, but that doesn't mean it isn't carrying vital information. Each time you consider a dream too mysterious to figure out, you are dismissing an important intuitive message. Moreover, two different people may receive identical symbolic images in a dream, but the meaning of those images may be completely different. If one person dreams about flying in a plane toward a certain destination, that symbolic image may represent an upcoming opportunity for fast forward movement. If someone else were to have the same dream about flying, his message might be to slow down and become more grounded and balanced. You'll become a real expert in dream interpretation after a little practice. Keep a notebook and pen by the side of your bed to briefly record the images you "see" when you dream. Then you may hone your interpretive skills at your leisure. To most quickly confirm the accuracy of your interpretations, you may communicate with your angels. Once you believe you have correctly figured out what a particular dream is meant to convey, simply ask your angels if you are on the right track. They will be very candid with you. If you have not correctly interpreted the dream, they will help you learn to decipher the symbolism, and in doing so, you'll access much more intuitive information than ever before.

QUESTION: What can I do if I feel so desperate or confused that I can't go on another day?

ANSWER: First of all, I want you to understand that you won't be able to move forward until you stop berating yourself for the "mistakes" you've made that have gotten you into this situation. By being self-critical, you're squandering precious energy that you could be investing in changing your life for the better. Next, force yourself to perform a simple exercise. I say "force" because I guarantee that you won't initially feel like doing anything besides feeling angry or sorry for yourself. But if you really want to feel better, try what I'm suggesting. Force yourself to sit down for a moment with a pad and pen. At the top of one page, write *Why I Hate My Life*. At the top of a second page, write *What I Would Like My Life to Become*. As you fill in the *hate* list, you'll build an awareness of what is making you so unhappy. As you fill in the *would like* list, you'll develop a list of positive goals that you can look forward to achieving. After you have completed a rough outline of both categories, put the *hate* list away in a drawer, and try to focus all of your attention on the *would like* list.

QUESTION: Why do I feel so miserable and depressed that I don't want to live anymore? I hate my life so much right now that I would do *anything* to feel better.

ANSWER: We all feel this way from time to time. Your suffering is most likely caused by the fact that you've gotten sidetracked from your spiritual agenda. If you're not happy or fulfilled, you've probably taken an unnecessary side road that is only leading toward depression.

QUESTION: How can I get back on track with my spiritual agenda so I can feel better and do something meaningful with my life?

ANSWER: My first recommendation is that you determine what your spiritual agenda actually *is*. If you are clueless about your destiny, you'll never be able to change your life. As you've already learned from reading earlier chapters of this book, there are two sources of information that you can access to learn about your spiritual agenda. The first source is your soul. The second source is your angels. You can reap incredible benefits by learning to tap into the wealth of personal information available from either of these sources. By doing so, you'll have unlimited access to the spiritual information that can help keep you on track and encourage your forward movement. Once you can retrieve information from your soul's memory, and speak directly with your angels, you'll never feel lost or alone again. To connect with your soul's memory bank, practice the simple technique described in chapter six. To open direct communication with your angels, practice the exercise I've described in the beginning of this chapter. In addition, you may want to consult my book, *How to Talk With Your Angels*, or one of the many other books available on channeling. I want you to understand that you *definitely* have the ability to communicate with both your soul and your angels.

QUESTION: I plan to practice your techniques, but developing my own ability will take *time*. I need information *right now* to get my life back on track!

ANSWER: Then I suggest you visit with a reputable channel who has the ability to access your soul's memory bank for you, and chat directly with your angels. An experienced channel can often obtain all the information within your soul about your life's work, issues you are meant to resolve, your spiritual contracts with others, your health and longevity, and even your experiences in past lives. But make certain that in your current state of desperation, you don't visit with a psychic or channel whom you don't know anything about. If you're going to trust someone to provide such personal information, please do your homework. Ask people you respect if they know of a good channel, or contact New Age bookstores in your area for a referral. If you visit a channel who won't tape their sessions, can't really explain the source of their information, asks for additional money on top of their normal fee, warns you only *they* can access intuitive information, pressures you to return for another session, suggests that you need to invest in candles, potions, or other cockamamie paraphernalia that they sell, or even mentions the word *curse*, run as fast as you can in the opposite direction. Don't spend any additional money with them, and consider it another good learning experience. If there is one message I've tried to convey in this book, it's that *you have the ability to access information on your own*. If you take the time to do so, you'll have the ability for the rest

you already have lung problems, you are tempting fate. If you are consuming alcohol and you already have liver problems, you are pushing the envelope. If you work in an environment teeming with dangerous chemicals, you are likely to be shaving years off your life. In terms of safety, particularly if you are a woman, every time you hear a little voice inside of you saying, ''There's danger in the parking lot! Don't walk to your car alone'' or ''Don't jog at night anymore'' or ''Your [ex]partner is going to make good on his threats of violence'' or ''Don't drink and drive'' you are receiving valuable, possibly *lifesaving* intuitive information. *Listen to it!* Stop thinking of this kind of intuitive information as *inconvenient* or *disruptive* to your normal routine! What could be more disruptive to your life than being raped or killed? Don't let that happen to you. *Listen to your inner voice.*

QUESTION: What if the intuitive information I receive is shocking or upsetting? I don't want to know about anything that's negative.

ANSWER: None of us likes to receive intuitive information that is initially baffling, hurtful, or disturbing, but it's a blessing that we can access not only what we *want* to hear, but also what we *need* to hear. Would you really want to remain in a cocoon of denial that could ultimately result in greater pain at a later date, or would you prefer to be *forewarned* about something so that you could prepare yourself emotionally? Wouldn't the intuitive information, in truth, be a great *blessing*, in that it could enable you to avoid a nasty surprise at a later date? For example, if you have a partner who is cheating, sooner or later you're going to have to face the reality that your relationship may end. Similarly, if you have a job that isn't secure, sooner or later you're going to have to face the reality of looking for a new job, and possibly experiencing financial difficulties in the process. If a situation like this already exists, or is likely to occur, wouldn't you want to know about it as soon as possible in order to protect yourself? Whenever we attempt to avoid or dismiss negative information by saying, "Well, that's just impossible to believe! It can't be right! If it were really true, I would already know about it! I don't want to even think about something that will cause me so much pain!" the usual response from our angels is often, "If you didn't *need* the information at this time, we wouldn't be *trying so hard* to deliver it to you! It's time to wake up and smell the coffee!"

QUESTION: If I learn to receive my own intuitive information, why would I need the services of a channel, no matter how good they are?

ANSWER: You *don't*, unless it is an unusually traumatic period in your life and you feel the need to get confirmation of what you've already received from your soul, or from your angels.

QUESTION: Do you believe in God? What are your religious or spiritual beliefs?

ANSWER: I have a very strong belief in God. I also believe that angels are heavenly messengers who help us accomplish as much as possible while we exist on earth. Our angels work right beside us, even if we are unaware of their presence. Many years ago, through my experience with channeling, I discovered that it is indeed possible to communicate with God, our angels, or any other spiritual being, as long as they wish to speak to us. Because angels are messengers from God, their communication with us is heavenly and divine. Therefore, it is nonsense that channeling with heavenly beings could ever be considered sacrilegious. We have to remember that we, too, are residents of the heavenly plane between our lifetimes here on earth. Our ability to communicate with the heavenly plane is a gift from God. We are meant to use this gift to build upon and develop our existing levels of spiritual enlightenment, so that we may complete as much of our earthly spiritual agenda as possible. As I shared in my first book, *How to Talk With Your Angels,* I was raised as a Catholic. While growing up and being exposed to a religion I found to be intolerant and judgmental, I continually felt unworthy and frightened. Every time I attended catechism or Mass, I would hear dire warnings about breaking the "rules" of the Catholic religion's very specific guidelines that dictate what a person should do, what a person should say, how a person should worship, and even what a person should think! As a recovering Catholic, I would describe myself as more spiritual than religious. My current philosophy is very simple. I believe each person should decide for himself whether to embrace a particular religion or form of spirituality. Most important, I believe that when an individual sets out to explore all the different forms of religion and/or spirituality, that he consider choosing the one(s) that help him feel good about himself and more connected with his fellow man, as well as the one that he finds most nurturing, uplifting, and recharging to his emotions and his spirit.

QUESTION: What if I keep receiving intuitive information that I can't relate to?

ANSWER: You are likely receiving intuitive information about an issue you are ignoring, or that you still have some work to do on an issue that you thought you had already resolved. Trust that you will *not* continue to receive intuitive information about something that you've already fully resolved or completed. If you keep receiving intuitive information about something, then rest assured that it's affecting your life *right now*, and it needs your immediate attention.

QUESTION: Is there any way my intuitive information could get mixed up with someone else's? Could I somehow receive information that was meant for another person?

ANSWER: When you develop your intuitive ability, you'll be consistently receiving angelic messages that will help facilitate your spiritual growth. You'll also be receiving intuitive information about friends, family members, and business colleagues that your angels feel would be of interest to you. From time to time, you may experience an episode of channeling with someone else's angel, who will ask you to pass along an intuitive message to another person who is spiritually closed or blocked. In such instances, you have the right to decide if you want to pass along that message. Whether you do so or not is entirely up to you, but if you choose not to, then the angels will keep contacting others who can channel, until the intuitive information is passed along via another human being. Unless you are a professional channel, you can very safely assume that most of the intuitive information you receive will be meant strictly for you, or a very close friend or family member. If you ever become confused about any intuitive information you receive, simply ask your angels about the meaning of the message, and if it was specifically meant for you. The more you practice your ability to communicate with your angels, the more detailed, comprehensive, and unmistakable the messages will become.

QUESTION: Is it possible to receive information from a bad, or dangerous spiritual being?

ANSWER: Without exception, all the angels with whom I've ever spoken all confirm that for a spiritual being to work in the capacity of an angel, he must meet certain unwavering criteria. First, he must be of an exalted level of enlightenment. Second, he must be willing to work tirelessly in the quest to protect and guide the human beings in his charge to greater levels of spiritual awareness. He must have the highest motives, and his integrity and honor must be above reproach. Because they remain invisible to so many people, and because human beings have a tendency to be closed to anything existing outside their five senses, I believe that working as a guardian angel is probably one of the most thankless, unrecognized, and torturous jobs in all of the universe. The angels have repeatedly told me that every single guardian angel must be sanctioned by a heavenly council, and then must "earn his wings" by spending a lengthy period of time in training with more experienced angels. You can trust that when you develop your channeling ability and communicate with your angels you'll be receiving intuitive information of the highest order that will be presented to you for your greatest benefit. The only other spiritual beings who would have access to you are your deceased friends and family members. If you do not wish to speak with them, all you have to do is tell them so, and they will refrain from contacting you.

QUESTION: If I'm on the right spiritual path, why am I so scared?

ANSWER: If you're on the right spiritual path, you are steadily moving forward toward your destiny. As you move forward through all sorts of transition, you'll have the opportunity to take a number of personal and professional risks. These risks will require a leap of faith, both in yourself, and in all the other people with whom you are associated. Making transitions always requires a leap of faith because while we have complete control over *our* behavior, we have absolutely *no* control over others. There are times when things turn out very differently than we had planned. Often, when other people don't honor commitments to us, we become hurt, angry, or disillusioned, and we may be scared to take similar risks in the future. But in order to achieve our spiritual destiny, we must transcend this fear. When you take significant risks, it's unrealistic to believe that you shouldn't feel frightened about what could occur in a future that holds no guarantees, no matter how spiritual or intuitive you are. I know it may seem ironic to you, but quite often I feel frightened about major shifts in my life, even though I have developed the ability to ''see'' what is most likely to take place before, during, and after a transition!

Author's Note

I AM PLANNING future seminars based on my books, *How to Talk with Your Angels* and *Discover Your Spiritual Destiny*, in a number of major cities. If you would like to share in the experience of building greater enlightenment, I welcome you to contact my office for more information.

Kim O'Neill Seminars
7745 San Felipe
Suite 206
Houston, Texas 77063
Telephone: 713-784-1122

Fax: 713-784-3434

FASCINATING BOOKS
OF SPIRITUALITY
AND PSYCHIC DIVINATION

CLOUD NINE: A DREAMER'S DICTIONARY
by Sandra A. Thomson
77384-8/$6.99 US/$8.99 Can

SECRETS OF SHAMANISM:
TAPPING THE SPIRIT POWER
WITHIN YOU
by Jose Stevens, Ph.D. and Lena S. Stevens
75607-2/$6.99 US/$8.99 Can

SUN SIGNS FOR THE NEW MILLENNIUM
by Geraldine Rose and Cassandra Wilcox
78942-6/$14.00 US/$21.00 Can

SPIRITUAL TAROT: SEVENTY-EIGHT
PATHS TO PERSONAL DEVELOPMENT
by Signe E. Echols, M.S., Robert Mueller, Ph.D.,
and Sandra A. Thomson
78206-5/$12.50 US/$16.50 Can

Amazing and Inspiring True Stories of Divine Intervention

ANGELS
by Hope Price
72331-X/$5.99 US

ANGELS AMONG US
by Don Fearheiley
77377-5/$6.50 US/$8.99 Can

MIRACLES
by Don Fearheiley
77652-9/$5.99 US/$7.99 Can

HOW TO TALK WITH YOUR ANGELS
by Kim O'Neill
78194-8/$5.99 US/$7.99 Can

MIRACLE ON THE MOUNTAIN
A True Tale of Faith and Survival
by William and Mary Hoffer
78979-5/$5.99 US/$7.99 Can

THE NATIONWIDE #1 BESTSELLER

the Relaxation Response

by Herbert Benson, M.D.
with Miriam Z. Klipper

A SIMPLE MEDITATIVE TECHNIQUE THAT HAS HELPED MILLIONS TO COPE WITH FATIGUE, ANXIETY AND STRESS

Available Now—
00676-6/ $6.99 US/ $8.99 Can